Attention Deficit Hyperactivity Disorder

Third edition

Is Attention Deficit Hyperactivity Disorder a 'made-up' term?

Is it simply an excuse for bad behaviour?

How do children with ADHD really experience school?

This practical teacher's guide dispels all the myth and gets down to the facts about ADHD. It explores the nitty-gritty of what you need to know in order to help the children in your class to cope with this complex condition.

This fully revised third edition gives an overview of the disorder based on the broad internationally recognised approach to ADHD, which takes account of its biological as well as environmental elements. It includes:

- real-life classroom scenarios and case studies of specific children;
- practical management strategies for both teachers and parents;
- an exploration of prevailing attitudes to ADHD;
- advice on initial diagnosis and ongoing assessment.

Packed full of no-nonsense advice and tips, this book will help you adopt the educational strategies and behaviour management approaches that are best suited to each individual child. It also explores the use of alternative treatments, such as psychological and psychiatric strategies, medication, counselling, coaching and changes to diet.

Children who have ADHD can often experience school failure, expulsion and emotional, behavioural and social problems. By demystifying the disorder and its coexisting conditions, this book will help you to understand and manage ADHD, enabling you to offer the children you teach a more positive future.

Geoff Kewley is a Consultant Neurodevelopmental Paediatrician at the Learning Assessment & Neurocare Centre, West Sussex, UK.

D0319264

nasen
Helping Everyone Achieve

Other titles published in association with the National Association for Special Educational Needs (nasen):

The SEN Handbook for Trainee Teachers, NQTs and Teaching Assistants
Wendy Spooner
978–0–415–56771–8

Young People with Anti-Social Behaviours: Practical Resources for Professionals
Kathy Hampson
978–0–415–56570–7

Confronting Obstacles to Inclusion: International Responses to Developing Inclusive Education
Richard Rose
978–0–415–49361–1 (HB)
978–0–415–49363–5 (PB)

Supporting Children's Reading: A Complete Short Course for Teaching Assistants, Volunteer Helpers and Parents
Margaret Hughes and Peter Guppy
978–0–415–49836–4

Beating Bureaucracy in Special Educational Needs
Jean Gross
978–0–415–44114–8

A Handbook for Inclusion Managers: Steering your School towards Inclusion
Ann Sydney
978–0–415–49197–6 (HB)
978–0–415–49198–3 (PB)

Teaching Foundation Mathematics: A Guide for Teachers of Older Students with Learning Disabilities
Nadia Naggar-Smith
978–0–415–45164–2

Dyspraxia in the Early Years: Identifying and Supporting Children with Movement Difficulties, Second edition
Christine Macintyre
978–0–415–47684–3

Dyspraxia 5–14: Identifying and Supporting Young People with Movement Difficulties, Second edition
Christine Macintyre
978–0–415–54397–2 (HB)
978–0–415–54396–5 (PB)

Living with Dyslexia: The Social and Emotional Consequences of Specific Learning Difficulties/Disabilities, Second edition
Barbara Riddick
978–0–415–47758–1

Attention Deficit Hyperactivity Disorder

What can teachers do?

Third edition

Geoff Kewley

Routledge
Taylor & Francis Group

LONDON AND NEW YORK

nasen
Helping Everyone Achieve

First edition published 1999
by LAC Press

Second edition published 2005
by David Fulton Publishers

This edition published 2011
by Routledge
2 Park Square, Milton Park, Abingdon, Oxon OX14 4RN

Simultaneously published in the USA and Canada
by Routledge
270 Madison Avenue, New York, NY 10016

Routledge is an imprint of the Taylor & Francis Group, an informa business

Typeset in ITC Stone Serif and Frutiger by RefineCatch Limited, Bungay, Suffolk
Printed and bound in Great Britain by MPG Books Group, UK

British Library Cataloguing in Publication Data
A catalogue record for this book is available from the British Library.

Library of Congress Cataloging-in-Publication Data
Kewley, Geoff.
Attention deficit hyperactivity disorder : what can teachers do? /
Geoff Kewley. – 3rd ed.
p. cm.
Includes index.
1. Attention-deficit hyperactivity disorder.   I. Title.
RJ506.H9K493 2011
618.92'8589–dc22   2010014022

ISBN13: 978-0-415-49202-7 (pbk)
ISBN13: 978-0-203-84172-3 (ebk)

Helping Everyone Achieve

nasen is a professional membership association which supports all those who work with or care for children and young people with special and additional educational needs. Members include teachers, teaching assistants, support workers, other educationalists, students and parents.

nasen supports its members through policy documents, journals, its magazine *Special!*, publications, professional development courses, regional networks and newsletters. Its website contains more current information such as responses to government consultations. **nasen**'s published documents are held in very high regard both in the UK and internationally.

Contents

Foreword

I came across a situation recently where I heard a teacher complaining that a boy with ADHD was using the label simply to excuse bad behaviour: 'This Attention Devastation Hyperactivity Disorder', he claimed, 'is just a made-up term'. He is, in fact, quite right as clearly he has not understood what the term ADHD actually means. If this is the case, how does he intend to understand the child he is working with?

He is also correct, however, in another sense because Attention DEFICIT Hyperactivity Disorder is not an excuse for inappropriate behaviour but instead an explanation of differences in learning and behaviour style. Individuals with ADHD, it is said, do not have 'a problem in knowing what to do but doing what they know'.

Explaining, understanding and helping to manage children and young people with ADHD is something that Geoff Kewley has been doing for over 35 years both in the UK and Australia. He set up the Learning Assessment & Neurocare Centre in Horsham, Sussex in 1993 and has in the last 17 years improved the behaviour and learning outcomes of literally thousands of children and young people.

Geoff and I first met in 1995 when I was a Deputy Head teacher and we have spoken at many events together over the years and, though he is a healthcare professional, he has always believed in and taken an active interest in the power of education and behaviour modification in terms of management of ADHD.

Geoff, in fact, also co-founded a school in his native New South Wales, Australia many years ago. He has always maintained close links with both the schools and children that teachers from the LANC have assessed, and treated over the years. As a result, Geoff has vast experience and expertise with regard to the strategies and approaches that can help children with ADHD both survive and succeed in the school environment.

In this third edition of *ADHD: What Can Teachers Do?*, Geoff does not preach good practice but instead he explains and clearly illustrates process and practice for teachers and schools. In addition, through a series of case studies of specific children, teachers will clearly recognise individuals that they meet daily in their classrooms.

In demystifying ADHD and coexisting conditions, and providing a range of both classroom- and non-classroom-based strategies for consideration, Geoff gets to the very heart of ADHD management. This is dealing with each of the three core areas of educational, behavioural and socialisation management.

This book provides the opportunity for all teachers who read, review and reflect on the strategies and solutions clearly described to improve the learning and behaviour outcomes for their students with ADHD.

Fin O'Regan
Educational Consultant

Preface

An appropriate understanding of ADHD and related conditions is now an essential requirement of any teacher with the significantly increased recognition and validity of the condition, especially since the report of the National Institute of Clinical Excellence in 2008, and also the increasing recognition of ADHD as a valid disability.

However, there has been a great deal of myth and misinformation regarding the basic nature of ADHD, and particularly of the medications used to treat it. This frequently has meant some teachers do not 'believe in' ADHD, or consider it to be an excuse for poor behaviour or 'laziness'. Notions such as: 'if children try hard enough they can concentrate just fine' and that behaviour problems are the fault of the parents and, with a right degree of educational and behavioural support, all children can be normal, have been erroneously widespread.

This book aims to bridge the gap between educational and medical perspectives, especially as the evidence base to the management of ADHD is that the most effective strategies are a combination of educational and medical strategies as appropriate.

The debate has now moved on and ADHD is recognised as a condition of brain dysfunction, probably involving multiple sites in the brain. It presents a wide variation of symptoms and difficulties within the classroom setting: some children are just inattentive, some are impulsive and inattentive, and in others the hyperactivity often lessens with time. Many children have other complications or conditions, the symptoms of which overlap and interlock.

Difficulties related to ADHD can present barriers to a child's learning and achievement. It is extremely important for teachers and other professionals working with children to understand how to manage it appropriately. In schools, a proactive approach to support learning and enhance the development of social skills and self-esteem can turn a negative situation into a very positive one. Much can be achieved where teachers and support staff, medical practitioners and parents collaborate well in the management of an individual child.

This book outlines clearly the core features of ADHD, along with the complications or coexisting conditions that frequently occur and which may impact on the classroom situation. It explains the rationale for the use of medication, and emphasises that this should be prescribed only after a comprehensive assessment. There is clear advice for teachers on educational strategies for the child with ADHD, and a 'troubleshooting' chapter considers specific situations that teachers may have difficulties dealing with. Above all there is emphasis on the reality of having ADHD, the validity of the condition and the fact that untreated ADHD represents a very considerable hidden handicap, but also that it is a very treatable condition, and that effective teaching can make all the difference to a child.

Acknowledgements

The team at the Learning Assessment & Neurocare Centre has developed many of the concepts in this book over the years since 1993. Particular thanks go to Pauline Latham for her never-ending supply of supportive ideas, constructive comments, tireless unofficial editing and clarity of thought regarding the various issues that are pertinent to different professionals and the families living with ADHD.

I would particularly like to acknowledge the many children and their families who have, by virtue of their various difficulties and my involvement in their long-term management, helped me to piece together the jigsaw of ADHD, which forms the basis of this book. The contrast between their difficulties prior to effective ADHD management and the delightful personalities and competencies that clearly show through once effective management is given is very gratifying and humbling.

Disclaimer

Every effort has been made to make the book as comprehensive as possible. This text is intended to educate and to act as a source of general information, relevant at the time of printing. It is not intended to be a substitute for specific professional services or consultation, nor as a means of making a self-diagnosis.

Profiles of 'typical' children with ADHD

Recognising ADHD

For teachers, a wide range of difficulties in the classroom can be the result of ADHD, although not always recognised as such. However, most teachers now recognise children with ADHD who may have variations on one of the three core ADHD symptoms: that is, often overactive in the classroom, disruptive and may have behavioural and/or emotional difficulties. Many children have the predominantly inattentive type of the condition which is better known as 'attention deficit disorder'. These children have difficulty in concentrating, are easily distracted, daydream, 'space out' and often tend to 'fade away' in the classroom rather than be disruptive. However, it is all variations of the same overall condition. Although the condition was originally thought of as just relating to hyperactive children, it is now recognised in recent years that any one of the three core symptoms of ADHD, i.e. impulsiveness, inattentiveness or hyperactivity, may be a problem and that each is equally important in its own way, causing the individual child significant problems.

Also, the broader concept of ADHD takes into account the fact that other coexisting conditions occur frequently with ADHD and compound the child's degree of impairment, e.g.:

- excessively oppositional behaviour;
- depression;
- specific learning difficulties;
- Asperger's Syndrome;
- low self-esteem.

The child may have a great deal of difficulty in paying attention and staying focused. Often such children are able to 'hyperfocus' on interesting tasks but 'do not do boring.' It is important that the diagnosis is not missed because of this 'on–off switch' creating marked differences in focus, which appear to be outside the child's volition. The child may be verbally impulsive and call out repeatedly in class. The coexisting conditions may mask the underlying ADHD so it is not always recognised, or they may mean that the difficulties are inappropriately put down to environmental or home difficulties. Consideration of the possibility of a child having ADHD always comes back to the question, is that child excessively inattentive, hyperactive or impulsive?

Children with ADHD, therefore, may have a wide range of difficulties – each child is very individual. However, there are some fairly typical threads to the most common variations of ADHD and these are illustrated in the case studies on the following pages.

CASE STUDY **Horace**

Horace lives in a blur of activity and noise. In nursery school his constant running about didn't matter so much, but now that he has to sit still longer in class he is always getting into trouble for being 'disruptive'. He talks incessantly at home and in class and is always interrupting, but these interruptions are never to the point. When he has friends round, he's the one being rowdy, not that he has many friends any more. The other children say he's nasty and doesn't stick to the rules when they play games. You can't let him go to the park on his own either; he's always falling out of trees or roller-blading on the busy road.

His parents say:

- 'He's like Tigger in *Winnie the Pooh* – always bouncing. We just don't know what to do with him.'
- 'We should have guessed he'd be like this: it was like a Manchester United football match while I was carrying him.'
- 'If he'd been our first, he would have been an only child.'
- 'What wears us down most is his non-stop talking. We never get any peace.'
- 'I tell him off for something and he goes and does the same thing again within two minutes.'
- 'He becomes bored so easily.'
- 'We have been through so many babysitters.'

His teachers say:

- 'If he wasn't in my class, life would be so much easier – he causes me more stress than the rest of the class put together.'
- 'He needs supergluing to the chair to make him sit still at school.'
- 'Everybody laughs at him – the other children set him up to do naughty things, yet he seems to have no real friends.'
- 'He is always calling out in class and often has his hand up, but rarely knows the answer.'

Horace says:

- 'I wish I was invited to parties more and had more friends.'
- 'It's all Mum's fault.'

Horace has Hyperactive/Impulsive ADHD.

CASE STUDY	Ingrid

Ingrid lives in a dream world of her own; if you are talking to her she looks right through you or switches off halfway through, especially if she's bored by the subject. She never gets around to starting her homework, let alone finishing it. She always has an excuse or she gets distracted by something else. If you ask her to fetch things you have to repeat yourself several times, and then she comes back with only one of the things. If it were up to her, she'd always be late for school and clubs. It's not that she doesn't want to go; she gets distracted and forgets the time. One day she can concentrate, especially if she's interested; the next day she loses her pencil case, forgets to pass on notes from school and takes hours to do one page of homework.

Her parents say:

- 'It's as if the lights are on but no-one is there.'
- 'We repeatedly ask her the same question and get no reply.'
- 'She could not even look into my eyes long enough to say goodnight.'
- 'She never has any idea where she has left things.'

Her teachers say:

- 'She needs to put her mind to it and take notice of what is happening in class.'
- 'She knows the topic but makes silly mistakes.'
- 'She seems to be drowsy during the day. Is she getting enough sleep?'
- 'Please make sure Ingrid brings her sports kit to school. I have had to excuse her twice this week from games.'
- 'She is a brilliant reader, but she can't be bothered to pick up a book because she can't concentrate.'

Ingrid says:

- 'I know I am not concentrating but I just can't seem to help it.'
- 'My friends tease me and say I am off with the fairies.'
- 'The boys say, "Well, you're only a girl, what does it matter?"'

Ingrid has Predominantly Inattentive ADHD.

<table>
<tr><td>**CASE STUDY**</td><td>**Gilbert**</td></tr>
</table>

Gilbert's parents had always known that he was very bright, and before he started school he could write his name, read books easily and understood a great deal of what was going on in the world. However, he never did well at school, and while he could put his energy into sport and other activities, where he was clearly very confident, in the classroom he was average in some subjects and below average in others. Although his parents were very concerned they were seen by the school as being over-anxious. His teachers found he could concentrate really well in some subjects, like Science and Information Technology, but in English, History and Geography, especially where he did not like the teachers, he did very badly indeed. He had difficulty in concentrating in those subjects but in other things he could over-focus.

His parents eventually transferred him to a private school with small class sizes and increased structure and support. Gilbert did very well for a while and was at the top of the year for the first two terms. However, he gradually slipped back to his old ways and was in the lower part of the year.

An educational psychology assessment showed he had an IQ of 140, putting him in the top 1 per cent of children. Thus he has tremendous ability.

His parents say:

- 'Gilbert has so much ability, yet he is often switched off and not with us and does not seem to concentrate very well.'
- 'He can concentrate on things like dinosaurs, computers and astronomy, in which he remains interested for hours and hours.'
- 'He knows so much about certain things – if only he would put it into practice, especially at school, and use his energy in the right direction.'

His teacher says:

- 'It's amazing how well he can concentrate on computers, but in English and Maths he just daydreams.'
- 'Although he is always looking out of the window, he always seems to know what we are talking about.'

Gilbert says:

- 'I don't know why I find it so hard. Some children seem to be able to get the work done in about half the time it takes me.'
- 'Having an interesting teacher makes all the difference.'
- 'I really don't think I'm very bright.'
- 'I find I get on better with adults.'

Gilbert is gifted but has ADHD.

CASE STUDY   **Melvin**

Although Melvin was a whirlwind as a toddler, and his mother cut the obvious trigger factors from his diet, she wouldn't regard him as hyperactive now that he is eleven years old. In fact his ADHD has been masked by the fact that he is so angry, defiant and easily upset, and he is getting into trouble for stealing, starting fights, hurting the cat and lighting fires. He has frequent outbursts, has virtually no self-confidence, has no friends, never gets asked to parties, doesn't get asked to play in the football teams because he has to play the rules his way, and his coordination is pretty poor. He now has a stutter which makes friendships harder. At school he is disruptive, easily distracted and is a long way behind. He gets some special needs help and his parents are hoping he will be given a Statement of Special Needs soon.

His parents say:

- 'I could have coped with his hyperactivity, but it is his anger, defiance and other behaviour that have caused so many problems.'
- 'He has been a handful since the moment he was born.'
- 'He even got excluded from preschool.'
- 'I am really worried that he is going to end up in jail.'
- 'He always says it isn't his fault. You can sit and watch him do something, but he still claims it is not his fault!'
- 'I don't know how I've coped without having to put him into foster care.'

His teachers say:

- 'If only he would stop and think before he answers questions in class . . .'
- 'He has been suspended three times and he will be permanently excluded next time. He is a danger to the other children in the class.'
- 'Mud sticks, and we tend to automatically blame him, though often the other children have put him up to it.'
- 'He has no sense of danger.'

Melvin says:

- 'I'm desperate to have friends, but they don't want to play with me.'
- 'I feel so embarrassed when I keep stuttering in class.'
- 'My best friend is the cat.'

Melvin's ADHD is masked by his coexisting conditions and complications.

Toby is a nine-year-old. Just before starting school it was noticed that he did lots of shoulder shrugging and face twitching and began to sniff more and more, and to cough and spit. Before that he had always been quite active, angry and argumentative and was quite a handful. At preschool he often hit the other children and was regarded as a whirlwind, and concerns had been expressed that he might not concentrate long enough to learn.

He was also quite obsessive; he needed to line his toys up exactly in the correct position. He insisted on using a certain cup and blue plate – he had to put the milk, then the sugar on his cereal in an exact way. If he had a routine for doing something and this did not happen, he could get very upset and have a 'stress attack'.

He was being teased about his tics at school, and tried so hard to control them that when he came home they usually became a lot worse. His neck tics were so bad he even saw the physiotherapist because of neck pain. His spitting was getting worse and he kept chewing holes in his jumpers.

His parents say:

- 'Once one habit stops, another starts almost immediately.'
- 'When he walks into a room he has to check everything. If he is interrupted he has to start again.'
- 'Certainly his tics have been a real problem, but it is his impulsiveness, his obsessions and his aggression that put so much pressure on the family.'

His teacher says:

- 'On a day-to-day basis it is his concentration, easy distractibility, rudeness and hitting other children that are the main problems.'
- 'Some days he seems to be quite depressed.'

Toby says:

- 'I am so tired of being teased by the other kids. I don't understand why I'm different.'
- 'I get scared when my body makes movements I don't want it to.'
- 'I try to make my [facial] tics into something normal like a cough or a yawn so that people don't think I'm odd.'
- [To his peers:] 'Do you think I like twitching like this?'

Toby has Tourette's Syndrome.

CASE STUDY	Alexander

Alexander has always seemed different, he had difficulty maintaining eye contact with his parents when he was younger, and his speech development was slow and indistinct. He didn't enjoy being cuddled and he has always needed a set routine, especially around mealtimes, going out and going to bed. He needs the same plate and fork; he needs to have the curtains drawn and the light on and his room and his toys arranged in a very specific way.

He doesn't really seem to need friends. He doesn't relate well to people and his communication skills are poor. He is also very active and cannot sit still for very long at school and does not stay on task well. He hits other children at random.

His parents say:

- 'Some professionals say he has autism, others say he is dyspraxic, and yet others say he is hyperactive.'

- 'We just feel that if he could only concentrate and stay on task a little he might cope better with his other problems.'

- 'We always have to be careful to do things the way we know Alexander wants them done, otherwise life is unbearable.'

- 'He hates change – even Christmas and Easter – and can't cope with surprises.'

His teachers say:

- 'I can't get my fingers close enough together to measure his concentration span.'
- 'It is better when he knows what is planned ahead, and when there is a routine.'
- 'He doesn't cope well with lunchtime or playtime.'
- 'Going to school for Alexander is a real act of courage.'

Alexander says . . .

. . . very little. He doesn't seem to care what happens. However, when it comes to dinosaurs, spacemen or his favourite cartoon:

- 'I know a lot more than anybody else.'

Alexander has ADHD and some features of Asperger's Syndrome.

CASE STUDY   Leslie

Leslie has always struggled at school because of developmental and speech and language problems. He was helped by Portage (a local service of therapists) to stimulate his development before he started school, and this was very useful. Even then it was noticed that he couldn't concentrate, that his speech development was slow and indistinct and that he tended to use the wrong words. He had been adopted, and his adoptive parents separated when he was six years old. He was said to be just like his natural father.

At school he couldn't stay on task and focus; he was in the language unit with the help of a small class size but he became more and more angry and defiant and was eventually excluded. His educational psychology assessment showed an IQ of 90 but with specific weaknesses in reading and spelling.

His parents say:

- 'We know he isn't particularly bright but we feel that if he could concentrate he could do a little better.'
- 'Although we are divorced now we noticed problems with him from one week old. We do not think our divorce is the cause of these, although it may have aggravated them.'
- 'School sees the bad work and the lack of homework, but they don't realise the hours of agony that have gone into doing it.'
- 'I was eventually asked not to bother taking him to school any more.'

His teachers say:

- 'Although he is not very bright, I think if he could concentrate he could do a lot better.'
- 'His speech is a lot better now, but he still has difficulty expressing himself.'
- 'In a one-to-one situation he improves, but in the main class he just cannot focus and he is distracted all the time.'

Leslie says:

- 'Nobody understands what I say.'

Leslie has ADHD and specific learning difficulties.

CASE STUDY	Ted

Ted is a teenager who had been expelled for starting a fire in the classroom. He was just starting his two-year GCSE coursework but his teachers suspect he won't finish it. Over the years there have been many difficulties. He had been suspended several times, usually for starting fights and being rude to his teachers.

His parents sought many professional opinions but generally have been blamed for his poor behaviour.

Ted has become increasingly frustrated over the years, has difficulty settling down to things and getting his homework done and really doesn't have the academic basis from which to start his coursework. Concentrating, for him, is very difficult and this has been noted in most of his school reports over the years. However, it has generally been the behavioural difficulties that have gained him most attention. When he was 12 he tried to hang himself and had been admitted to the local psychiatric hospital. Ted is starting to get into trouble outside school, has been taken to the police station several times for stealing from shops and joyriding in cars. He has received several cautions and his parents are very concerned that, especially now he is no longer at school, he will end up in major trouble. He has been drinking alcohol and has experimented with cannabis. He is never at home, he can't sit still and do nothing or watch television; he has to go out with his friends.

His parents say:

- 'When he was younger I was told he wasn't hyperactive enough to get help.'
- 'We just don't feel we can trust Ted.'
- 'He has some friends but they are always the wrong types. He gets into bad company.'
- 'We know he has the ability, but he just doesn't settle down to anything.'
- 'He just has no motivation any more.'
- 'He is a real Jekyll & Hyde – loving one minute and completely upset about something the next.'
- 'Underneath it all is a lovely child trying to get out.'

His teachers say:

- 'Ted is just lazy and should try harder.'
- 'If he hits anyone else he will be expelled permanently.'
- 'I don't know how he is going to settle down to the GCSE coursework.'

Ted says:

- 'I wouldn't mind being a lawyer, because you get paid to argue.'
- 'I really just don't care any more.'
- 'I can't understand why I can do some things and not others.'
- 'School is a real drag; I just want to get out and get a job.'

Ted's ADHD was diagnosed late as a teenager.

What is ADHD?

Although it is a medical condition of brain dysfunction, ADHD significantly affects educational performance. It is estimated to occur in 3% to 5% of school children, and is a very common condition in the classroom. At least one child in every 20, i.e. one to two children in each classroom, may have ADHD. The condition can cause difficulties in the classroom in a wide range of ways and in some cases can be difficult to differentiate from normal behaviour. It therefore behoves teachers to have a very good understanding of the condition.

In the past decade there has been increased recognition that ADHD is an internationally recognised condition. The difficulties must be pervasive and persistent and must significantly interfere with the child's everyday life.

Girls tend more frequently to be inattentive and to daydream, and they tend to fade away in class without their problems necessarily being acknowledged. In the past, teachers have sometimes had difficulty in accepting that such children are not just lazy and could concentrate if they tried harder, or could try to have better self-control. Such concepts are subtle but are very important to understand in the context of ADHD. To many teachers, excessive difficulty with the child calling out, not concentrating or being active may just appear to be an extreme personality issue; however, if it is persistent the possibility of ADHD should be considered.

For more about the management of ADHD, see Chapter 4.

Many children with ADHD have complications and these include:

- **Excessive oppositionality**: i.e. these children always blame someone else – it is never their fault, they are defiant, they lack the ability to respect the moral authority of the teachers, they are emotionally volatile, they argue, and they refuse requests. Of course all teenagers can be oppositional some of the time; however, the early onset of Oppositional Defiant Disorder in association with ADHD, as well as the normal oppositionality of puberty, can cause a great many difficulties.

- **Disruptive behaviour disorders**: i.e. not only excessive oppositionality and mood volatility, and antisocial behaviour, this may involve getting into frequent fights, arguments, verbal confrontations and problems with rule-governed behaviour.

- **Anxiety or depression**: children may feel that their life is not worth living, that they wish they were dead, and in particular may become extremely demoralised. They may also worry about getting the work wrong, about socialising, and about a wide range of things. These can lead to self-harm if not effectively managed.

- **Specific learning difficulties**: this is a much broader concept than the simplicity of the term 'dyslexia". Specific learning difficulties can involve reading, spelling, maths, and, whilst they may be associated and cause concentration difficulties, when the concentration difficulties coexist with specific learning problems the child is doubly disadvantaged.

- **Obsessions**: such as storing and saving things, wanting to have things just so, have routines and excessively set ways of doing things. Obsessions sometimes occur in combination with both vocal and motor tics. They may also be part of a child's autistic spectrum difficulties such as Asperger's Syndrome, with or without coexisting ADHD.

- **Developmental coordination difficulties (dyspraxia)**: problems with spatial awareness, motor planning, poor pencil grip and problems with gross motor difficulties such as ball catching or bike riding may coexist with ADHD.

- **Auditory processing difficulties**: for some children the problem is not so much of concentration difficulties but of difficulty in processing what they hear. Things go in one ear and out of the other. Auditory processing problems can coexist with ADHD.

- **Speech and language problems**: sometimes this is because of auditory processing problems or difficulties in retaining what one has heard or wanted to say. Some children with ADHD speak extremely rapidly and indistinctly. Others have difficulty in getting to the point and can be quite loquacious or have problems with taking things too literally.

These complications frequently mask or camouflage the underlying ADHD core symptoms, which can make accurate diagnosis, assessment and recognition of a child's problems quite difficult. However, if concentration or self-control difficulties persist, the diagnosis of ADHD should be considered, irrespective of the child's socioeconomic status.

ADHD often runs in families – it appears that genetics and biology tend to create a vulnerability that can be compounded by difficulties in the child's environment. The child's parents should not necessarily be blamed for the difficulties but rather it should be appreciated that many children have innate difficulties which cause problems, and that parenting such a child is often very difficult and stressful, with these children putting very significant pressure on their families.

The copious myths and misinformation about conditions such as ADHD, and the medications often used to treat it, that are sometimes used as part of their management, have made it very difficult for teachers and parents to gain factual information on the condition and the best way of helping an individual child.

Therefore, in one way or another, ADHD is an eminently treatable condition. It is very important for teachers to recognise the condition early on in a child's schooling, so that strategies that have been shown to be helpful, such as behavioural management and medication, can be put in place.

Children with ADHD generally behave about a third younger than their chronological age. This means that a 16-year-old will need to be treated in much the same way as a 12-year-old in many ways. Whilst many children with ADHD, especially the very bright ones, have strengths and weaknesses within that profile, their lack of maturity, their impulsiveness, their educational underachievement and their social skills difficulties do mean that it is helpful to think of them as a younger child and thus to have more realistic expectations of them.

ADHD is a biologically based disability that results in educational and behavioural as well as other difficulties. It is treatable but not curable. Educational strategies and teachers' interventions can have a very positive and powerful effect on the refractory nature of ADHD; however, the refractory nature of the condition does mean that very often these children will have ongoing difficulties in their academic and social lives despite all the help they are able to get.

Remember that very frequently ADHD is only one part of an individual child's complex difficulties. He or she may also have associated specific learning difficulties, social skills difficulties, family problems, organisational problems, depression, oppositional behaviour or some features of autistic spectrum difficulty.

By having a good understanding of ADHD, teachers are in a much better position to effectively teach and care for the child with a condition. Prior to starting to teach a child it is helpful to try and ascertain the child's individual profile, his or her strengths and weaknesses, and how the condition of ADHD specifically impacts on his or her learning and behaviour, as well as whether or not there are other difficulties. Generally it is helpful to give more frequent and more salient positive consequences for actions and behaviours and to give more consistent negative consequences and accommodations if necessary. Also acknowledge that it is harder for ADHD pupils to do the same academic work and show the same degree of social behaviour as would be expected of other pupils.

Children with ADHD tend to benefit from much more immediate and salient consequences. It is generally worthwhile getting into the habit of using immediate consequences regularly in their management. Aim to use positives before negatives if possible. Try and develop accommodations and positive strategies to minimise the occurrence of the negative behaviour. If something goes wrong try and discuss with the child subsequently how this could have been prevented and discuss a possible scenario that may help things go better in the future. However, such children with ADHD are less likely to learn through previous experience and tend not to remember or readily assimilate past experiences.

Ways in which ADHD may be drawn to the teacher's attention

Professionals today fortunately tend to differentiate between ADHD and ADD. Although part of the same overall condition, it makes more sense for teachers to differentiate between the more inattentive children who may have ADD, and the more hyperactive, impulsive and disruptive children who more likely have ADHD.

However, children with ADHD/ADD may present in a wide range of ways, but generally tend to fall into one of four groups:

1 **Hyperactive only**

   Those, usually fairly young, children who are still extremely active.

2 **Mainly impulsive, hyperactivity diminishes with time**

   In many children the hyperactivity has diminished with time but they remain inattentive and impulsive, and frequently have other complications as time goes by. These children may worsen their self-esteem and social skills, and may become demoralised. They develop a bigger gap educationally from their peers, and may become increasingly disruptive and antisocial. Often it can be deceptive and, because the hyperactivity has lessened, some people fall into the trap of thinking that all the child's problems have gone away, this clearly not being the case.

3 **Predominantly Inattentive ADHD (often known as ADD)**

   These children have Attention Deficit Disorder, but are not hyperactive or impulsive. They are spaced out, daydreamy and inattentive. There is a subgroup now – those with 'sluggish cognitive tempo' – who are particularly demotivated and 'switched off'. They may not be noticed by teachers, especially if they are bright as this tends to mask the problems. Research suggests that if attention deficit disorder were more fully recognised, the incidence in boys and girls would probably be more equal.

4 Core symptoms present but masked on a day-to-day basis by the coexisting conditions

For example, in some children with ADHD, the associated learning difficulties, oppositional behaviour, conduct disorder, poor social skills, low self-esteem and other difficulties can overshadow and mask the underlying ADHD symptoms. Of all the groups, this one is often under-recognised. These children are often excluded from school without their condition being recognised.

Causes

Attention Deficit/Hyperactivity Disorder frequently runs in families. International research, using various scanning techniques, links ADHD symptoms particularly to differences in brain wave activity in the forebrain, an area associated with concentration, time awareness and impulse control. There seems to be a malfunction in the brain's neurochemical messengers that regulate these traits.

> If one child in a family has ADHD there is:
>
> - a one in three chance of each subsequent child having ADHD;
>
> - a 30–50% chance that one or other parent has the condition.

Genetic, brain-imaging and psychological research have started to converge to develop a theoretical model of ADHD as largely a problem in response inhibition. Abnormalities of brain structure and function, generally involving the fronto-striatal pathways, have been shown by brain-scanning techniques. These studies are complemented by genetic studies showing heritability and, more recently, specific gene abnormalities, especially involving the dopamine system. ADHD epitomises this.

Many professionals and, to a large degree, society in general have tended to attribute children's behavioural problems to purely psychological or social problems, often complicated by poor parenting, teaching or environmental factors. However, in recent years the increase in evidence that there is a biological basis for much of children's behavioural and educational difficulties has meant a change in thinking regarding the causes of these problems.

In looking in more detail at the core features of ADHD and getting a better understanding of what is significant and what is not, research suggests that the basic problem in ADHD lies in inhibiting inappropriate behaviour and controlling impulses. Its core features are inattentiveness, hyperactivity and impulsiveness. For a diagnosis of ADHD to be made, there can be inattentiveness alone, hyperactivity and impulsiveness alone, or all three features together. Any assessment must be thorough and comprehensive and include information that is obtained from the school. Such children often live for the moment and do not think of the future difficulties. An assessment must ascertain whether the behaviour is:

> Core features:
>
> - inattentiveness
> - hyperactivity
> - impulsiveness.

- causing difficulties for the child in two or more settings, but not necessarily all the time;
- causing excessive and significant interference with everyday life;
- inappropriate for age and developmental level;
- not due to any other reason; and

- present for at least six months, and usually has become obvious before seven years of age.

The essential features of ADHD are outlined in the Diagnostic and Statistical Manual of the American Psychiatric Association and are discussed below. There are nine inattentive criteria and nine hyperactive/impulsive criteria. In either case, six of the nine criteria must be met for a diagnosis to be made.

Inattentiveness

Everyone can be inattentive at times, but children who have inattentiveness as part of their ADHD, usually have significant difficulties which are recurrently commented on at school and sometimes at home. Children with other conditions such as dyslexia or speech and language problems tend to be inattentive more in the academic setting whilst those with ADD tend to be inattentive in most settings.

About a third of children with ADHD have never been hyperactive and their main problem is inattentiveness. Others may have been hyperactive or overactive when younger, but this has decreased with time, while their concentration and distractibility difficulties persist at school.

'Concentration is the supreme art because no other art can be conceived without it – whilst with it anything can be achieved.' (*The Inner Game of Tennis*, W. Timothy Gallwey)

'A notable feature in many of these cases . . . is a quite abnormal incapacity for sustained attention. Both parents and school teachers have specially noted this feature as something unusual.' (G. F. Still, 1902)

Hyperactivity

Diagnosis of hyperactivity requires careful evaluation of everyday behaviour in school and at home, not just in the consulting room on the day of assessment. Only a small proportion of children diagnosed with ADHD in clinics are actually hyperactive during the assessment.

While hyperactivity is very frequently a major problem for children with ADHD, it is important to recognise that excessive inattentiveness and impulsiveness can be equally problematic. Sometimes parents consider that they can manage a child's hyperactivity, but it is the impulsiveness, inattentiveness and other complications that are more problematic for the child. Hyperactivity frequently becomes less obvious as the child gets older.

'He needs supergluing to his seat.'

'He can always find an excuse to sharpen pencils or go to the toilet and just can't sit still in class.'

'He bounces off the walls.'

Impulsiveness

Excessive impulsiveness means that the child acts, speaks or has an excessive emotional reaction without thinking. Many scientists feel that the basic defect in many children with ADHD is their difficulty in inhibiting behaviour and the inability to stop and reflect prior to acting. Impulsiveness results in going for the most immediate goal or reward – physically, verbally or emotionally. These children have difficulty in complying with rules and tend to push boundaries and limits.

Verbal and emotional impulsiveness cause difficulty with teachers and peers. Normal discipline and other forms of behaviour management are much less likely

'The serious danger which these children constitute to both themselves and to society calls for active recognition.' (G. F. Still, 1902)

to work for these children, because they continue to act without forethought and cannot learn from their mistakes. They do the same things over and over again, as a reflex action.

Poor social skills can be aggravated by physically inappropriate touching, clowning and doing silly things, and being socially out of tune. Many ADHD children are 'set up' by other children at school who know that they are able to trigger impulsive behaviour and that the child will act inappropriately and be the one who gets into trouble.

> 'The degree of moral control which may be perfectly normal in a very young child, may be altogether below the average for a child a few years older.'
> G. F. Still, 1902

To make a diagnosis of signficant inattentiveness in association with ADHD the following are relevant

These children:

- **often fail to give close attention to details or make careless mistakes in schoolwork or other activities**. Things are missed out that the child clearly knows; silly mistakes occur, especially when a subject or teacher is perceived as boring. They may have jumped words or paragraphs or just scanned the words. They tend to rush their work to finish it quickly, irrespective of quality.

- **often have difficulty sustaining attention in tasks or play activities**. They have difficulty sustaining attention and are easily distracted. They may find it hard to filter out extraneous sounds. Bright children, in particular, may focus intensely on some things that interest them but have little or no concentration for others. This does not mean that their concentration control is wilful; rather that their brains are unable to reach the concentration threshold required for apparently boring work.

- **often do not seem to listen when spoken to directly**. They seem not to listen and in class are often lost in a world of their own, missing much of what is going on. At home and in conversations they often switch off and are seen as rude and unappreciative. They frequently look straight through you and can thus appear quite antisocial in conversational style. They can sometimes be misdiagnosed as autistic because of lack of eye contact, and thus lack of communication. Parents know that they have to get their message across early in the conversation. The possibility of a child having auditory processing difficulties either as part of the ADHD or separately should be considered.

- **often do not follow through on instructions and fail to finish schoolwork and chores (but not because of oppositionality or failure to understand)**. They fail to finish schoolwork because they get distracted and bored. They cannot be asked to fetch more than one thing at a time; they will start things and not finish them, often because they are distracted by something else.

- **often have difficulty organising tasks or activities**. Although they often know where items are beneath the piles of things in their bedrooms, children with ADHD live in the 'here and now'. They have difficulties managing time and in thinking and planning ahead. They may forget appointments, arrive late, not have planned their day, week, month or even their next minute. Their inability to appreciate time and to think ahead is felt to be an extremely important aspect of ADHD and one that creates many difficulties for the child. It is often difficult for teachers to recognise that the organisational abilities that the rest of the class take for granted are very difficult for these children.

- ***often avoid, dislike or are reluctant to engage in tasks that require sustained mental effort (such as schoolwork or homework)***. Actually engaging the brain in mental activities is very hard. The chronic procrastination is extremely frustrating for parents and teachers. It can sometimes take several hours to engage the child in five or ten minutes' homework because of this difficulty. They find multiple excuses, such as going to the toilet, sharpening pencils, etc. and, very often, homework time is the cause of much argument in the household. Teachers may fail to appreciate the effort that has gone into a small amount of homework.

- ***often lose things that are necessary for tasks or activities (e.g. toys, school assignments, pencils, books or sports equipment/kit)***. Loss of concentration, and distractibility, means that children with ADHD tend to lose things that they need for schoolwork and other activities. They put something down and move on to the next thing, or they daydream and get distracted.

- ***often are easily distracted by extraneous stimuli***. Some children with ADHD seem to have difficulty in filtering inputs – so the teacher's voice is not easily differentiated from the birds singing in the trees, the boy whispering behind or the music playing next door. However, other such children are able to concentrate better in a noisy environment. They are very easily distracted. Many children with ADHD are also distracted by their own thoughts – especially children with high IQs who often pick up the gist of what is going on in the classroom very readily but then switch off to focus on something that is much more interesting to them. The inability to stay on task for more than a brief period of time may make the child appear disruptive in class.

    This variation in the ability to concentrate, depending on the situation, is important diagnostically. Whereas children without ADHD are able to make themselves concentrate on 'boring' things, children with ADHD have difficulty with this; they tend to have more difficulties in listening skills than in visual concentration skills.

- ***often are forgetful in daily activities***. Children with ADHD have a poor short-term memory. They forget to pass on phone messages, miss outings and forget their homework. They often have enormous trouble in starting things, put things off and have great difficulty in getting organised for work or school. They tend to need to re-read things. They see the words but they do not seem to take them in. They can be drowsy in the daytime, and their work is often inconsistent with very good and bad days. They often have real problems with short-term working memory and so they tend to forget what they are just about to do, much more so than do other people.

Hyperactive criteria

These children:

- *fidget*. Many children become less hyperactive with time and by the age of 9 or 10 may be just fidgety. Fidgeting (sometimes called 'rump hyperactivity') can, nevertheless, be very annoying.

- *frequently leave their seat in class*. This is often not noticed in younger children, because the class management allows more moving around (sharpening pencils, going to the toilet, etc.). However, as the child gets older he or she is not able to roam around, and this can cause difficulties and make him or her appear wilfully disruptive.

- *often run about or climb excessively in situations in which it is inappropriate*. Especially as preschoolers, hyperactive children are always running, often climbing and getting into dangerous situations without any forethought.

- *have difficulty playing or engaging in leisure activities quietly*. Many hyperactive children are more noisy than average.

- *are often 'on the go' or act as if 'driven by a motor'*. This is the classic description of hyperactive children, especially preschoolers, but it often becomes less of a problem, or is modified in different ways with time.

- *often talk excessively*. The 'verbal hyperactivity' of these children is often one of the most exasperating features for parents. They ramble on, frequently about nothing of any relevance. However, if asked to talk about something specifically and stick to the point, they often have difficulty with appropriate verbal expression. This is probably a difficulty in executive function, and in organising speech.

Other common features

- *Male–female differences:* Hyperactive girls tend to have more difficulties with mood swings and emotional outbursts and tend to be less aggressive than hyperactive boys. However, when these aggressive and conduct problems occur, they can be extremely hard to cope with.

- *Early masking:* The symptoms of some children with ADHD may be masked at nursery school because of the high levels of activity allowed there, and the intense supervision. The high energy levels appropriate to their age may be hard to distinguish from hyperactivity. However, problems may still be occurring at home, where there is less structure. Many mothers say that their child was hyperactive in the womb, was very restless and never really seemed to sleep, and that this behaviour continued immediately after birth.

- *Sleep patterns:* Parents may have been told that their child is not hyperactive because they sleep well. However, by no means all hyperactive children have problems in getting to sleep. Many hyperactive children sleep well, often burnt out by the whirlwind activity of the day, especially if they have risen early in the morning.

Impulsive criteria

The criteria are that the child:

- blurts out answers before questions have been completed;
- has difficulty awaiting his or her turn; and
- interrupts or intrudes on others (e.g. butts into conversations or games).

This means that they have difficulty with:

- ***Verbal impulsiveness****:* These children interrupt conversations (much more than normal children) and shout out in class, even though often they do not know the answer. They may say cruel and hurtful things to their friends without appreciating the damaging effect their comments may have, leading to resentment and poor relationships.

- ***Physical impulsiveness****:* The child acts without forethought and seems to have no idea of cause and effect, they live for the moment. For example, he or she may run on the road to chase a ball or to see a friend on the other side, without considering the danger. He or she may jump out of a window or pretend to be Superman, or climb a tree without thinking about how to get down. The child may frequently be a danger to him or herself, although parents have developed strategies to cope with this and to protect the child.

- ***Emotional impulsiveness****:* Children who are emotionally impulsive have marked mood swings and temper outbursts, often for little or no reason. This may be difficult to differentiate from oppositional defiant behaviour (see pages 25 and 29), and frequently the two coexist. They may get upset very readily but forget about their tantrums quickly and then wonder why others are feeling upset, angry or resentful. Such episodes are usually short-lived and last no longer than five minutes. Frequently the child has come back to normal whilst others are still upset.

A diagnosis of ADHD is made by thorough assessment of the symptoms, discussion as to their relevance, the obtaining of information from the school, and the assessment that these symptoms are significant. Rating scales can be very helpful but are not essential and a diagnosis should never be made solely on the basis of rating scales. In whichever way the assessment is done, the bottom line is that the assessor should be very clear that the symptoms are significant, and they are impacting on the child's life and progress.

Consideration of IQ: low intelligence and gifted/talented

At the extreme, children with lower IQs generally find it more hard to concentrate, but if their concentration difficulties are out of proportion to their learning problems the possibility of ADHD should be considered. Treatment may enable them to function better and to achieve to their full ability. Sometimes children with low ability and very poor concentration appear, after treatment, to have more reasonable ability, which has been obscured by the ADHD and complicated by specific learning difficulties.

At the other extreme, many children seen in ADHD clinics are of above-average intelligence. In school their intelligence often appears to enable them to compensate for their ADHD adequately to put in an average academic performance, though this may be significant and unrecognised underachievement compared to their potential. Even if teachers identify this, these children do not usually qualify for special help as they are often considered to be simply lazy. Sometimes it is the child's low self-esteem or behavioural problems, largely because of boredom, that can be drawn to the teacher's attention.

Such children tend to focus intensely on subjects that interest them, or when they like the teacher, but under-focus when they consider a subject or teacher boring. They often achieve well in a test or one-to-one situation, and often thrive on complexity. However, they tend to be easily distracted in group work or more open-ended tasks. In a supportive school they may cope well and their condition might only show up when they reach the more pressured and less structured environment of A-level courses, college or university.

Many very bright children are often extremely aware of their failings and tend to struggle, with some becoming very oppositional when they get bored; others have very high expectations of themselves and struggle with this, whilst there is a group of very bright children who can cruise on their intelligence and seem very laid back about it. Many such children deserve to be not only on the gifted and talented register but also on the special needs register. In many ways they can be seen like a mountain range with extremely significant strengths but also 'valleys' of difficulties with weak concentration, organisation problems, low self-esteem, etc.

These children do have an enormous ability to be creative and to think laterally and, if handled correctly, they become extremely effective adults. However, the effort required for each achievement is much greater than for someone without ADHD. On the other hand, being gifted with ADHD and having associated obsessive tendencies can make for great achievements.

> 'The teachers used to say that they had never seen such a bright pupil. They even gave her GCSE work when she was 12 years old, but it was so hard to keep her on task.'

> 'Subjects that hold his interest on a one-to-one level fail to engage his interest in a group situation.'

> Quotes from Winston Churchill's school reports:
>
> 'His persistent lateness is disgraceful.'
>
> 'If he were to really exert himself he might yet be first at the end of term.'
>
> 'He loses his books and papers and various other things.'
>
> 'He is so regular in his irregularity that I sometimes think he cannot help it.'
>
> 'He has such good abilities made useless by habitual negligence.'

Growing up with ADHD

The exact symptoms of ADHD, their severity and the course the condition takes depend on many factors, including educational and social circumstances. Although originally seen as a condition of childhood, in the past decade it has been realised that as a biological condition affecting brain function, ADHD is present throughout life. With time, environmental problems tend to exacerbate, and by adulthood the core ADHD symptoms are frequently buried under complications such as depression, anxiety and oppositional behaviour. One of the most prevalent myths about ADHD is that it disappears at puberty. While hyperactivity often decreases by that age, many of the other difficulties are generally still present or worsening. ADHD symptoms persist into adolescence for 80% of children with ADHD and into adulthood for 60%.

The report of the National Institute of Clinical Excellence (September 2008/ www.nice.org.uk) was extremely helpful in validating the importance of ADHD. However, it particularly emphasised that it was a condition not only of childhood but also of adolescence and indeed adulthood. Thus very many children with ADHD do not outgrow their condition and may have significant problems in the later adolescence and adulthood.

Very young children with ADHD

Key features of ADHD in young children

- Some young children show symptoms of ADHD from a very early age.
- It can be difficult to differentiate between normal active preschool children and those that are hyperactive.

Effective management can reduce stress levels for the child and the teacher.

'Even though he's only two, his most common word is "No." '

Some children show ADHD symptoms in the early weeks of life, even in the womb. This usually indicates extreme hyperactivity, often with a very poor sleeping pattern, or the early onset of persistent oppositionality and even Conduct Disorder (see pages 26 and 62).

For primary school teachers, it is important to recognise that there are critical key features of ADHD in adolescence but by the time children with significant ADHD have entered senior school, they have often become very demoralised, and the transition from the more structured primary school to a senior school where there are many more organisational demands on them can be very difficult indeed. This is particularly so in very bright children.

'He's so active I just don't know how he'll be able to sit still when he starts school.'

It may be hard to differentiate between children with ADHD and other normal children of the same age who are usually extremely active anyway. However, studies suggest that most children who are eventually diagnosed as hyperactive were showing problems by 18 months.

'He's such a livewire I just can't get babysitters to look after him.'

Many such children show hyperactivity and behaviour problems at school. The extent to which a child's problems are due to difficult temperament or parenting problems is often very hard to decide. A child with a difficult temperament can make even the most skilful parents feel incompetent and discouraged. Also, one or both parents may have ADHD; resulting problems such as multiple job or relationship changes are, inappropriately, thought to be the sole cause of the child's problems.

While many preschoolers have problems with mood swings, in socialising and with high activity levels, if these problems persist and cause problems during this period an early assessment should be sought. Early assessment and effective management can markedly reduce stress levels in the child, the classroom and the family.

ADHD in adolescence

Key features of ADHD in adolescence

- Hyperactivity often diminishes by puberty.

- Physical impulsiveness may diminish, but verbal and emotional impulsiveness may increase.

- ADHD in adolescents is often masked by other factors, such as oppositionality, learning problems, low self-esteem, poor social skills, anxiety or depression.

Although hyperactivity has often declined by puberty, the other core ADHD symptoms – inattentiveness and impulsivity – remain. Physical impulsiveness may have lessened by this age, but adolescents with ADHD are likely to be much more verbally and emotionally impulsive. They will interrupt conversations, speak out of turn and lose friendships because of inappropriate remarks. They explode and have frequent tantrums, and often seem immune to rational and reasoned argument. For some with ADHD their problems with rule-governed behaviour mean that they push the limits, argue a lot, have difficulties with behaviour at school, are frequently excluded and may have problems with the law.

As the years go by, a child's underlying ADHD is frequently masked by complicating factors, particularly oppositionality, learning problems, low self-esteem and poor social skills. By the time the hormonal changes of puberty occur, life is extremely difficult. Motivation has usually diminished after years of persistent failure, and is often very low by adolescence. Lack of persistence and failure to follow rules and instructions also become very prominent features at this age.

Adolescents with ADHD show a wide variety of life patterns. At one extreme are those with Conduct Disorder, who may embark on a life of crime. Others have quite reasonable social skills, thrive on a great deal of stimulation, are the life and soul of the party and have reasonable, if superficial, relationships. Others may have underachieved academically, have low self-esteem and poor social skills, and be anxious, depressed or obsessive.

> 'He puts more pressure on the family than the other three children put together.'
>
> 'If only he would learn from his mistakes!'

Teaching adolescents with ADHD

The variation in the type and intensity of problems means that no two students are likely to show the same symptoms. Teachers and other professionals involved, as well as parents, have to cope with many different manifestations of teenage ADHD and should not expect to find a single, simple solution. These students do not necessarily respond to normal management strategies and therefore tend to be criticised and punished more, leading to hardened attitudes on both sides. Teachers need to be particularly adept at using general management strategies for a wide range of children with ADHD and this requires resources of time and energy that are often in short supply.

In the past, adolescents who did not easily adapt to rules or the requirements of higher education could leave school at 15 and find an occupation suited to their ability. Now GCSEs involve a large number of coursework assignments, over which it is all too easy for those with ADHD to procrastinate, and the exams require them to plan ahead and to concentrate on subjects that they may not find interesting. They are therefore a real test for both the teenager with ADHD and their teachers.

Many ADHD teenagers make progress only after they leave school and start on a career which is more to their liking, and where they can modify their lifestyle to maximise their strengths. Hyperactive teenagers may channel their energies into high-risk or emergency service jobs. Others successfully negotiate the world of computers and information technology. Those with a higher IQ, and who were less severely hyperactive and more emotionally stable as young children, tend to have a better outlook, as do those with better social skills, higher socioeconomic status and a supportive home environment with emotionally stable parents.

Common problems for adolescents with ADHD

- **Oppositionality**. More common in those with hyperactive/impulsive core symptoms, this is very persistent and can greatly harm relationships.

- **Conduct Disorder**. More common in those with Oppositional Defiant Disorder. Both girls and boys who go on to develop Conduct Disorder at this stage are at high risk of early involvement with the police and social services. Girls are sometimes misdiagnosed because their behaviour is generally not viewed as seriously as that of boys.

- **Anxiety and depression**. More common in those with predominantly inattentive ADHD. Manic depression occurs occasionally and should be considered if there are mood swings from very high to very low.

- **Poor social skills**. These are exacerbated by associated speech difficulties, oppositionality, mood swings or learning and language problems. Issues with self-esteem and social skills may be the greatest day-to-day problem for gifted teenagers with ADHD, and one of which they are very aware. Often their high IQ has enabled them to perform adequately until now.

- **Frustration**. Teenagers with ADHD become very frustrated, particularly by their day-to-day difficulties in their ability to perform. Their condition is beyond their control, but is frequently misinterpreted by others as wilful. Struggles in complying with rules, whether set by adults or their own peer group, add to their frustration.

- **Demotivation**. The daily struggle for adolescents with untreated ADHD of attending school, having difficulty socialising and the other complications, means that sometimes the mountain they have to climb is just too high. As a result they give up, becoming demotivated and demoralised. This is frequently one of the most difficult aspects of untreated ADHD to manage effectively.

- **Need for stimulation**. Those who are hyperactive with ADHD may have a low boredom threshold and flit from one high stimulation activity to another. This may be an element in cases of compulsive gambling and shopping, crime, substance abuse and teenage pregnancy.

- **Drug and alcohol abuse**. Studies show that 30–40% of adolescents with Conduct Disorder or manic depression and ADHD are subject to drug and alcohol abuse. Inattentiveness, excessive impulsiveness and a lack of awareness of the consequences of their actions, sometimes aggravated by substance abuse, contribute to the higher incidence of motor vehicle accidents in adolescents.

- **Teenage pregnancy**. Girls who have ADHD with excessive impulsiveness and low self-esteem have a higher chance of becoming pregnant as teenagers.

- **Suicide**. The combination of excessive impulsiveness and depression in some teenagers with ADHD may well trigger a suicide attempt and contribute to the high incidence of teenage suicide in the UK (two deaths per day). The lack of full appreciation of the consequences of their actions and the poor or impaired recollection of past experiences, together with their shorter-term view of the future and lack of awareness of time, may all increase the possibility of suicide.

ADHD in adults

'When I used to
work as a nurse
they called me
"Super nurse"– I
like being in the
thick of the action
and used to ask
for the most
difficult and
exciting jobs.'

'I couldn't count
the number of
jobs he has had in
the past ten
years.'

Between 70%
and 80% of
children with
ADHD have
persistent
difficulties into
adulthood.

ADHD in adults

■ Adult ADHD is
a real and often
disabling
condition.

■ It contributes to
workplace and
relationship
difficulties, and
antisocial
behaviour.

■ Some adults
with ADHD
manage to
use their
hyperactivity
and ability to
think laterally
to their
advantage.

As mentioned earlier, the fact that ADHD may progress into adulthood has only recently been fully realised. Between 30% and 50% of children diagnosed with ADHD have at least one parent with the condition, and other members of the extended family may also have ADHD. The varied patterns of presentation of ADHD in teenagers continue into adulthood, resulting in an even wider variation in the ways people present with, and cope with, the condition.

ADHD can be a particular problem with university entry. Transition from a reasonably structured school situation into the more mature and less structured situation at university can be very difficult for people with ADHD especially if they have significant executive function difficulties. They are usually very bright, but have a poor concept of time and great difficulties with organisation. They benefit from being put in touch with the university's Special Needs Department where in most universities significant supports such as a mentor, use of a laptop, and recording devices are available.

The effect of ADHD on society as a whole is increasingly recognised. Many adults have lived for years undiagnosed or misdiagnosed. ADHD contributes to workplace difficulties, divorce and relationship problems, job loss, unemployment, substance abuse and compulsive gambling. It greatly increases the risk of ending up in prison, and of underachieving generally. There are also the costs of the continuing provision of relatively ineffective services.

The range of problems for adults with ADHD varies enormously. Some remain very inattentive and as a result underachieve significantly in life and in the workplace. Others have persistent hyperactivity and impulsiveness and are more likely to be involved with antisocial behaviour and with substance misuse. Many of the ADHD symptoms verge on personality features and disorders. However, when they are significant, the possibility of the adult having ADHD needs to be considered. Frequently this means that, because of the genetic nature of ADHD, one or other or both parents may have features of the condition.

Adults may present with concentration problems, absent-mindedness, inappropriate decisions, mood swings, low self-esteem, significant workplace and relationship difficulties, and problems with substance misuse. Adults with ADHD have a much higher incidence of car accidents and speeding fines, of poor financial management, of dietary difficulties, of having more accidents generally, and of problems with their own parenting. They may have difficulties in following through on things, in achieving academically appropriately and in being disorganised, with poor time management.

The 2008 report of the National Institute of Clinical Excellence confirmed that ADHD is not just a childhood condition that in many cases affects the whole of the lifespan. For teachers the main difficulty clearly arises in the school setting; however, for many people the most troubling times for those with ADHD are in their late childhood years, entering sixth form college and going on to university or starting in their jobs. The increasing lack of structure, the peer influences, problems in organisation, and demotivation mean that in late adolescence and early adulthood a great many difficulties can occur. Because ADHD is a strongly genetic condition frequently the child's parents also have the condition. University lecturers, and those in other adult teaching institutions, must be aware of the implications of ADHD, and especially the possibility that it may have been masked by the person's giftedness.

Coexisting conditions

A number of other conditions have been found to coexist with ADHD and form an extended Attention Deficit/Hyperactivity Disorder syndrome. These conditions are more likely to occur in children with ADHD, complicating their symptoms and increasing the risk of psychiatric, educational and other problems. Disruptive behaviour disorders such as Oppositional Defiant Disorder or Conduct Disorder are relevant to teachers because of the persistent behavioural problems and the increased risk of school exclusion in this group. These complications are more common in people with combined or hyperactive/impulsive ADHD, while those with inattentive ADHD are more likely to have associated depression, anxiety and learning difficulties. Whether one condition causes the other, or vice versa, or whether they are just more likely to occur together, is as yet unclear.

At least two-thirds of those diagnosed with ADHD also have one or more co-existing conditions, and the later the diagnosis, the more likely these are to occur. This chapter describes the most common conditions.

Oppositional Defiant Disorder (ODD)

Between 40% and 60% of children with ADHD develop ODD by adolescence. Whilst most children, and particularly adolescents, are oppositional some of the time, in these children the oppositionality is persistent and excessive, occurring a lot of the time, every day and in many situations. At least 25% of children with ODD also have Conduct Disorder. Home difficulties and low socioeconomic problems and other environmental disadvantages may exacerbate the development of ADD.

Key features of children and adolescents with ODD

- They are often excessively hostile, defiant and argue frequently.
- The early onset of ODD has pernicious and devastating effects on such children who are usually more oppositional at home than at school.
- They lose their temper often.
- They refuse to comply with adults' requests or rules, go out of their way to annoy people and are frequently very touchy and readily annoyed.
- They may be excessively angry and resentful, or spiteful and vindictive.
- They tend to blame everyone and everything else for their mistakes.

Life with these individuals is like walking on eggshells and symptoms frequently worsen with time, in a vicious spiral of academic and relationship failure, with consequent lowering of self-esteem.

Conduct Disorder

- 40–60% of children with ADHD develop ODD; 25% of children with ODD also have Conduct Disorder.
- More than 90% of children and adolescents with Conduct Disorder have associated ADHD and Oppositional Defiant Disorder.
- They may be callous and unemotional, lack empathy and have problems in interpersonal relationships.
- They may have a superficial charm, but with little show of emotion and a lack of conscience.
- They tend to be excessively aggressive to people and animals, with problems involving the destruction of property, deceitfulness or theft and serious violation of rules; are often confrontational: bullying, threatening and intimidating others, starting physical fights or using weapons to cause serious harm to others.
- They may engage in overt antisocial activities such as fighting and causing physical harm.
- They may be involved in covert activities such as stealing.
- They may steal while confronting a victim, and may force the victim into sexual activity.
- They may have destroyed property or set fires – are often fascinated by flames and matches.
- They tend to break rules regularly, to stay out at night, to run away and to play truant.

In early-onset CD, problems start in childhood and the child develops significant difficulties before age 10 that are much more likely to persist throughout life.

In adolescent onset CD, occurring after 10 years of age, the difficulties are often limited to adolescence.

Children with emotional behavioural problems tend to get into more fights, they are more likely to be excluded and more likely to be in trouble with the youth justice system. Some may be shown to have bipolar disorder which is excessive, severe mood swings, a strong tendency to depression, and to severe rages.

- 10% of children with ADHD suffer from depression.

- 25% of adolescents with depression have a history of ADHD.

Depression

As many as 10% of children with ADHD suffer from depression, which can vary in severity from a moderate mood change, known as dysthymia, to a more severe change, with major depression or, occasionally, bipolar or manic depressive disorder.

Twenty-five per cent of adolescents with depression have a history of ADHD. Clearly, children who have attempted suicide need to be assessed for depression and coexisting ADHD. Adolescents who commit suicide have much higher rates of bipolar disorder and ADHD than those who attempt suicide. The impulsiveness associated with ADHD is extremely concerning when associated with severe depression.

Children with **dysthymia** tend to have:

- low mood on most days;
- poor appetite (or sometimes overeat);
- sleep difficulties;
- low energy;
- low self-esteem;
- concentration difficulties;
- a feeling of hopelessness.

Conditions that commonly coexist with ADHD

- Oppositional Defiant Disorder
- Conduct Disorder
- Depression
- Anxiety Disorder
- Obsessive Compulsive Disorder
- Sleep difficulties
- Learning difficulties
- Speech and language difficulties
- Tics
- Tourette's Syndrome
- Asperger's Syndrome
- Coordination difficulties
- Substance abuse.

Other common problems

- **Poor self-esteem**: despite lots of encouragement and lots of positives, self-esteem usually stays low.
- **Poor social skills**: these children usually very much want friends but things go wrong.
- **Insatiability**: going on and on about things, often driving teachers and parents to distraction.
- **Variability**: these children tend to have particularly good and particularly bad days for no obvious reason. This can make teaching them very difficult without a clear reference point.

- **Excessive dogmatism**: these children particularly see everything as either black or white and seem to have a cognitive difficulty in seeing other people's point of view.
- **Time management and organisational problems**: difficulties with planning, organisation and time management, the concept of time tends to be lacking and such children are often very late for things.
- **Relationship difficulties** particularly with peers and family. It can be because of a range of issues, not reading social situations, being dogmatic, being impulsive and not listening.
- **Demotivation**: in many children the persistence of effort in the presence of so many severe difficulties becomes overwhelming and they give up.
- **Problems with rules**: they tend to push the boundaries, to not respect authority, and to be defiant.
- **Over-sensitivity**: this can be to sound, as well as to touch, smell and taste.
- **Vulnerability to stress**: situations such as a divorce, death, and other family or life stresses tend to be coped with less well by a child with untreated ADHD.
- **Short-term memory problems**: these can affect writing things down from the board, in retaining information about what is learnt, and should be differentiated from a complete lack of understanding.
- **Soiling and wetting**: these are more common in people with ADHD and may frequently improve after treatment.
- **Physical symptoms** such as tummy ache or headache are more likely and are often a result of the stress of having untreated ADHD.

Children with major depression tend to have:

- low or depressed mood most of the time;
- marked loss of interest or pleasure in most activities;
- lost weight;
- sleep difficulties and be agitated;
- fatigue;
- feelings of worthlessness;
- difficulty in concentrating;
- recurrent thoughts of death and suicide.

Bipolar disorder

This should be considered in children with severe ADHD when there are multiple complications and/or persistent irritability and prolonged and aggressive temper outbursts. Young children may not have the mood swings from mania to depression characteristic of adults, and thus may be difficult to diagnose accurately. Bipolar disorder should be considered in any child with mood instability and oppositional symptoms particularly if there is a family history.

Pointers include:

- a family history of manic depression;

- severe and early onset of core ADHD features;
- Oppositional Defiant Disorder;
- Conduct Disorder with significant learning disabilities.

Anxiety Disorder

Those with ADD have some symptoms of anxiety. Children with Anxiety Disorder may:

- become anxious with change, especially over new situations or places;
- have problems with social or interpersonal failures;
- have fears, panic attacks or otherwise debilitating anxiety problems;
- have a fear of failure in the classroom and will be reluctant to try new things.

Obsessive Compulsive Disorder

Obsessions and compulsions are frequent in children with ADHD, and most common in those with coexisting Asperger's Syndrome (pages 1, 31 and 59) and Tourette's Syndrome (pages 31 and 60). Breaking the obsessions or compulsions, especially in preschool children, may cause significant defiance, tantrums and behavioural upsets which can be mistaken for purely Oppositional Defiant Disorder behaviour.

Children with excessive obsessive symptoms may:

- need to have their bedrooms organised in a fastidious way with their toys 'just so';
- have obsessional eating habits, needing specific cutlery and crockery;
- demand that items around the house are positioned in specific places;
- like and need routines;
- indulge in compulsive hand-washing or other cleansing activities.

Sleep difficulties

Many children with ADHD have sleep difficulties which can aggravate an already difficult situation, making the child tired and less able to concentrate during the day.

Children with sleep difficulties may:

- be very active all night and keep moving in their sleep, which is fitful and restless;
- be unable to sleep because of anxiety over noise, darkness and other disturbing conditions;
- be unable to get to sleep because their brains are active and they cannot relax.

Specific learning difficulties

About 30% of children with specific learning difficulties have associated ADHD.

Previously, the term 'dyslexia' has tended to be used as an all-embracing term for children with specific learning difficulties. Dyslexia can cause concentration difficulties in the educational setting only.

There is therefore a world of difference between stating that a child's concentration difficulties are caused by his or her dyslexia as distinct from a child having innate difficulty. Effectively managing the child's concentration problems can make the child available for learning.

In children with ADHD and coexisting learning difficulties:

■ the ability to learn is doubly compromised by poor concentration; such children are at exceptionally high risk of failure;

■ there may be difficulties in reading, spelling, numeracy or written expression;

■ there may be auditory short-term memory and auditory processing, or in some case central auditory processing disorder (severe problems in learning from listening, sounds localisation and lateralisation, and discrimination and recognition of auditory input) coexisting with the child's ADHD.

Speech and language difficulties

■ 30% of children with ADHD have, or have had, speech and language difficulties.

■ 30% of children seen initially for speech problems have ADHD.

■ 65% of children with both speech and learning difficulties have ADHD.

Significant speech and language problems, especially stuttering, can have a major impact on a child's self-esteem and socialising ability. Previously it was assumed that all concentration problems in children with speech and language difficulties are due to their frustration and struggle with speech problems. Speech and language therapists need to keep in mind the likelihood of associated ADHD. Children with more severe language problems, especially when there are obsessions and difficulties with social skills, may sometimes be difficult to distinguish from those with Asperger's Syndrome.

Children with ADHD may have:

■ delay in normal speech development;

■ lack of clarity;

■ problems in sequencing and problems in structuring what they want to say;

■ problems in verbal expression;

■ stuttering, hesitations and stammering;

■ difficulty with finishing sentences;

■ semantic pragmatic language disorder (misunderstanding of the subtleties of language).

Tics

Tics are sudden, rapid, repetitive movements or vocalisations and they commonly occur in association with ADHD. They can be made worse by stress and anxiety, and may fluctuate with the situation, coming and going for months at a time. Some children 'release' their tics once they come home from school, having been able to contain them during the school day.

Sometimes, if both vocal and motor tics are frequent, persistent and significant, a diagnosis of coexisting Tourette's Syndrome (see below) should be considered.

There is a wide range of tics:

- recurrent eye, face and shoulder movements;
- simple vocal tics: sniffing, coughing, grunting, hissing, barking, yelping, humming and other noises, spitting;
- more complex vocal tics: swearing, repeating their own or other people's words or phrases;
- simple motor tics: head and shoulder nodding and turning, finger tapping, wrist and finger flicking, leg twitching, foot stamping, shoulder shrugging, eye rolling and blinking, mouth opening, tongue poking, face pulling, grimacing, arm and leg stretching;
- more complex motor tics: grooming the hair or other parts of the body, touching objects or body parts, pinching or picking skin, retracing footsteps, copying others' actions, various facial and other gestures, turning round in circles, doing deep knee bends, hopping, jumping, skipping or rude finger and hand gestures.

Tourette's Syndrome

This condition is frequently associated with other neurological, emotional and behaviour difficulties, such as ADHD or Obsessive Compulsive Disorder. It is a disinhibition disorder best known for the associated swearing, although this occurs in only 10–30% of children with Tourette's Syndrome. The diagnosis of Tourette's Syndrome has tended to have a stigma attached to it, and it is frequently more practical to regard such a child as having ADHD with coexisting tics, and treat all aspects appropriately.

> 50–80% of people with Tourette's Syndrome also have coexisting ADHD.
>
> Only 10–30% of children with Tourette's have compulsive swearing problems.

Children with Tourette's Syndrome may:

- have persistent, multiple vocal and motor tics occurring in bouts, usually many times a day, but not necessarily, with vocal and motor tics occurring at the same time;
- have tics that occur intermittently but are persistent for several months at a time;
- suffer distress or impairment in social, occupational or other areas of functioning, because of their tics;
- swear ritualistically and compulsively, repeating words over and over again;
- make finger signs, dirty drawings or write dirty, and suffer from mental coprolalia (thinking excessively vulgar thoughts).

Asperger's Syndrome

A large group of children who will have Asperger's Syndrome do not have it as a pure condition, but may have features of both this and ADHD. These children frequently have the core symptoms of ADHD, i.e., hyperactive and impulsive

'One might mention a curious trait that is noticeable in some of these children, namely solitariness. The child shows no inclination to associate with or make friends with other children, and although apparently perfectly intelligent, shows a complete lack of natural affection, so that its parents seem hardly more to it than any stranger might be.' (G. F. Still, 1902)

and/or inattentive, but are also often obsessive and have rituals. It is therefore important to be aware of the tendency to misuse the terms of Asperger's Syndrome and ADHD. It is much more important to differentiate out the core symptoms. Some of these children are diagnosed as autistic when younger, and at other times they have schooling socialising difficulties, language disorders or ADHD. Some will first appear to have manic depression in adolescence or may only be diagnosed as adults. This is particularly a problem in secondary school settings.

In Asperger's Syndrome, the child does not really desire to share or socialise, whereas children with ADHD want to have friends and want to socialise, but they get it wrong.

Children with Asperger's Syndrome may have:

- (most) a relative lack of empathy;
- poor social skills;
- lack of need for reciprocal interaction, a tendency to be aloof;
- problems in developing age-appropriate peer relationships;
- poor use of non-verbal communication, for example lack of eye contact;
- difficulties in using language for communication, though in some, expressive language is superficially perfect;
- obsessional behaviour, particularly involving repetition and abnormal perseverance;
- a limited range of interests;
- delayed speech and language development;
- a very pedantic way of speaking, with peculiar vocal characteristics; and
- impaired understanding of speech, interpreting comments too literally.

Coordination problems

Handwriting improves in 80% of children with ADHD when treated medically, as do ball-catching and other gross motor skills.

Children with significant coordination difficulties are considered to have dyspraxia or, more appropriately, developmental coordination difficulties.

Problems with both fine and gross motor control are very common and are frequently diagnosed as dyspraxia. Any child with a 'dyspraxic' diagnosis who also has significant concentration or overactivity problems should also be assessed for coexisting ADHD.

Children with coordination problems may have:

- fine motor control problems: difficulties with handwriting, threading needles and stringing beads;
- gross motor control problems: problems in riding bikes and catching balls, generally tripping over things and being awkward; and
- apparent clumsiness that can be due to impulsive movement or lack of concentration.

Substance abuse

Substance abuse is much more likely in those with ADHD, especially if there is associated Conduct Disorder and/or manic depression. It has been suggested that substance abuse in ADHD is unwitting self-medication, as initially the drug or alcohol involved helps them concentrate and cope. Excessive impulsivity may also play a role.

- Experimentation with drugs appears to lead to abuse more rapidly in those with ADHD and at a younger age.
- The family histories of children with ADHD frequently reveal adults who are excessively involved with drugs and alcohol and whose history seems to suggest underlying ADHD.

> 30% of adults diagnosed with severe drug and alcohol abuse are estimated to have a childhood history of ADHD, usually with Conduct Disorder.

Poor self-esteem

Self-esteem is defined as feeling and believing in your own competence and worth. Good self-esteem enables you to tackle challenges, learn from both success and failure and treat yourself and others with respect. Poor self-esteem results in an inaccurate assessment of your own abilities and a lack of confidence. Especially in the classroom setting, children who are sensitive by nature, particularly if they are bright, tend to rapidly lower their self-esteem. The teaching style, the ability to develop the child's 'islets of competence', and to be constructive but sensitive in criticism is a very important teaching strategy.

The level of self-esteem is one of the crucial factors in determining what sort of problems children with ADHD will take through with them into adulthood. It is therefore crucial to develop strategies to protect and enhance the child's self-esteem.

Children with ADHD and low self-esteem:

> 'How can they believe in themselves if nobody else believes in them?'

- sometimes seem to have been born with low self-esteem despite a good environment;
- underachieve academically and socially during the early school years, decreasing self-esteem;
- may feel that they are stupid, even if their intelligence tests show that they are very bright and gifted;
- may get into a vicious circle, avoiding tasks to avoid 'failure', sometimes by disruptive clowning, or by not finishing them; and
- may lack confidence in social relationships.

Poor social skills

Children with ADHD want friends but get the social dialogue wrong. They know what to do, but are unable to put it into action; it is a performance problem rather than a total lack of skill. They may be set up by other children to do silly or dangerous things and may do so to try and establish friendships. Children with ADHD very much want friends, they want to be involved in parties and after-school activities but they get the social skill wrong. They are too close, too dogmatic, too 'in your face', and misread social cues. If they also have difficulties with coexisting Asperger's Syndrome they may need additional support in the playground.

Gifted children with ADHD frequently seem aware of their failure, and lack of social skills may be their most obvious symptom, as their high intelligence may initially enable them to function reasonably well academically. Social skills problems in adolescence may isolate the child from his or her peers. These difficulties may persist into adulthood.

Children with ADHD and poor social skills may:

> 'Apart from his cousin's, he has never, ever been invited to a birthday party.'

- have few, if any, friends;
- be excessively bossy, unsociable and/or impulsive;
- play with either much younger or much older children, rather than their peers;
- find group situations difficult and be better in one-to-one relationships;
- misinterpret the most innocent comments of others;
- never have been asked to friends' houses, even if their parents have repeatedly asked friends around;
- have relatively good superficial social skills, but get bored with long-term friendships and have difficulty forming deep and intimate relationships.

ADHD characteristics that cause problems with social skills

- Inattentiveness: switching off or daydreaming during conversations, misreading body language and social cues.
- Impulsiveness: getting too close and being 'in your face'.
- Physical impulsiveness: clowning, hitting, touching and other annoying mannerisms.
- Verbal impulsiveness: upsetting others by careless remarks.
- Emotional impulsiveness: getting upset for minor reasons, having tantrums or storming off.
- Hyperactivity: not staying still long enough to have a conversation.
- Verbal hyperactivity: blocking the reciprocal conversations that lead to friendship and cooperation.
- Short-term memory problems: forgetting what has happened previously in their relationship with a particular person.
- Insatiability: annoying other people by doing or saying the same things over and over again.
- Excessive depression, tenseness and anxiety, oppositionality and aggression may compound interpersonal relationship problems.
- Coordination issues, speech and language problems, especially stuttering and stammering and lack of clarity and language usage problems may further exacerbate social difficulties.

Insatiability

Children with ADHD may go on and on about things, or become 'stuck in a groove'. Reasonable responses seem to make little difference, as it becomes an obsession and the child seems not to hear the answer.

'He goes on and on and on about the most minor things, and drives me to distraction.'

Variability

Children with ADHD frequently have marked variation in their symptoms over hours, days or weeks, and some experts regard this as one of the most common features of ADHD. It seems to be unrelated to management techniques or any other clear cause and may possibly be related to overall neurotransmitter variations.

Such variability makes management very difficult for teachers. Unfortunately, children tend to be judged by their good days. On their bad days they are often reminded that they could do it previously, but it needs to be remembered that this variability is outside the child's control.

Excessive dogmatism

Children with ADHD very commonly see things as either 'black' or 'white' and find it hard to see and acknowledge another person's point of view. They appear to have a 'cognitive blindness.' This may make rational and reasonable argument difficult as they appear stubborn and unable to compromise. They may take an argument from a second or third stage in a sequence of events, failing to acknowledge the original problem, often because they have forgotten it due to their poor short-term memory.

Time management and organisational problems

A poor concept of time is a difficult one for teachers to always recognise in the children that they teach. Time management is the sort of thing that is taken for granted, yet it causes so many difficulties in a person's life. Poor time awareness and management is a hallmark of ADHD. Children with ADHD tend to 'live for the moment'. The deferment of tasks or rewards, or thinking about the past and the future, does not come easily. The inability to plan for the future, to think about the next hour or the next day, and to reflect on the past affects many aspects of their lives, especially planning and organisation. However, if they also have obsessional tendencies, this may help to counteract their time organisation problems.

Relationship difficulties

Living with a child with ADHD, especially if there is associated oppositionality, puts great stress on family relationships. However, in the past such relationship difficulties have often been seen as the primary cause of the child's problems. Where one or both parents also have ADHD symptoms, and so find it hard to use the ADHD behavioural management strategies, the problem could appear to be 'poor parenting'. Siblings also suffer, and there is no doubt that being a sibling of a child with ADHD causes enormous stress and strain in the relationship. Many siblings need support in their own right.

Demotivation

In children and adolescents struggling with untreated ADHD, drive and motivation diminish over the years. They persistently underachieve or have difficulties with tasks that really should be within their grasp. By their teenage years, many are lethargic, cannot be bothered to do anything, find it hard to engage in tasks requiring mental activity and procrastinate. For many children it is 'a mountain too high to climb.' The continuing stress of struggling with various difficulties of ADHD means that some children give up and opt out of school or situations. Parents often feel they have lost the preschool child they knew, who has become demoralised with long-standing struggles.

Problems with rules

Children with ADHD frequently push the boundaries to the limit. They tend to confront any sort of authority, partly because of their impulsiveness and partly because of not concentrating on what they are told to do. For example, many children with ADHD have no respect for their head teacher or other people and authority.

Over-sensitivity

Children with ADHD are frequently hypersensitive and also very sensitive to touch, smell, noise and a wide range of other stimuli. This is known as sensory integration disorder and can cause a great many difficulties for the child, such that the child can often appear to be obsessive in an effort to avoid things that he or she knows will make it worse. Many children also are hypersensitive to auditory input and noise in the classroom or a loud teacher's voice can again cause distress. They often do not enjoy being touched or cuddled, even as babies, and small amounts of sensory input may upset them greatly and cause tantrums and emotional outbursts. Labels on clothes, types of fabric, subtle smells and minor changes in their environment may not be well tolerated.

Vulnerability to stress

Untreated ADHD and its complications can adversely affect a person's ability to cope with life's stresses, such as death, divorce and other traumas.

Short-term memory problems

Many children with ADHD have short-term memory problems, especially in retaining and processing information from auditory input. Often visual information is processed better, unless there is associated dyslexia.

'It goes in one ear and out the other.'

Soiling and wetting

Some children with ADHD have problems with soiling and wetting; low self-esteem and daydreaming may be factors here. This may mean that the child becomes teased because of wetting or soiling. These symptoms often improve when the ADHD is effectively managed.

Physical symptoms

The stress of having untreated ADHD can manifest in recurrent headache and abdominal pain. Recurrent or persistent coughing or sniffing may be due to a vocal tic, rather than to asthma or nasal inflammation.

3 Assessment of children with ADHD

Teachers faced with a child who is persistently disruptive, who has poor concentration and is easily distracted, or who has possibly even been suspended or excluded from school, should consider ADHD as a possible cause of this. Teachers should have sufficient insight and awareness of ADHD to be able to alert parents that it is a possible reason for the behaviour. Parents can then choose to seek a specialist assessment to establish whether or not their child has ADHD. Schools are increasingly looking at ways of identifying or screening for ADHD at a young age. Although an accurate diagnosis should only be made by an experienced clinician, teachers and parents can become well-informed about the condition and its core symptoms.

When parents and/or teachers raise the possibility of a child having ADHD, it is essential for a comprehensive assessment to be made by an appropriate specialist. While the referral to that specialist should come from the family's GP, information from the teacher is essential in the assessment. It is helpful if teachers write a letter to the GP, including some facts to support the request for an assessment. The teacher will subsequently be contacted by the specialist clinic, usually to complete a rating scale form and also to supply any other information that they may have on the child. It is also helpful for previous teachers to give information on their perception of a child if possible.

> Available data from the report of the National Institute of Clinical Excellence suggests that in 2008, ADHD was both under-diagnosed and under-treated. Based on an incidence of 1% of UK school children being diagnosed as hyperkinetic, fewer than half of these were being adequately treated with medication. When the broader ADHD diagnostic concept is used, a figure of 3–5% of UK schoolchildren having this condition is usually suggested. This means that there is at least one child with ADHD in every classroom, and currently, therefore, very significant under-recognition.

The educational psychologist's role in the assessment is to evaluate the child's cognitive processes. If possible, the EP assessment should be done within the school setting, but otherwise it can take place at the specialist ADHD clinic. Whether or not the school educational psychologist becomes involved early on generally depends on local resources. If the teacher and/or special needs coordinator (SENCO) are concerned about a child, it is important to involve the school educational psychologist early.

Who is involved in the assessment?

The assessment should be undertaken by a medical specialist experienced in the complexity and wide range of presentations of ADHD, and should consider whether or not the child has ADHD. The differing core symptoms and complications mean that a child with the condition can present in a wide range of ways, and the condition can also be masked by complications and by the passage of time. A comprehensive assessment will exclude other conditions that can mimic ADHD and differentiate the symptoms from those caused by normal development and environmental difficulties.

The assessment should involve the people who spend most time with the child – the teacher and the parents. Teachers do not generally need to attend the assessments in person, although it is sometimes helpful if they are able to. Of course, the family should be consulted on this. However, information from teachers, both orally and in writing, is an essential part of the assessment process. The assessing professional does not necessarily need to sit in the classroom, as the child always gets to know that he or she is being watched. However, unbiased teacher feedback via the various teacher feedback forms in rating scales is an essential part of the assessment process. A diagnosis cannot be made without this.

Diagnosing ADHD for the first time in the teenage years is difficult, because the core symptoms are usually overshadowed by other coexisting conditions, and the condition itself has progressed for so long. Previous management strategies may have failed because of the unrecognised ADHD, leaving the teenager and the family discouraged. At this age, the individual must be willing to cooperate; by this stage some adolescents have become so oppositional and conduct-disordered that they are likely to refuse help.

The assessment and management strategies for ADHD are closely linked, and a thorough assessment should include discussion of the management options.

The family interview

The aim of the family interview is to enable the specialist to compile a well-documented history of the child's symptoms. Most clinicians will send a history interview form to the family several weeks before the interview appointment to enable the family to focus their minds on and discuss the key issues. This assessment questionnaire forms the basis of the interview and looks at the key problems worrying the child and the family, parents' ideas of the possible causes of the problems, what attempts have been made to resolve them in the past, and what help has been sought.

> The essential parts of a comprehensive assessment include:
>
> ■ family interview;
>
> ■ child interview;
>
> ■ medical examination;
>
> ■ educational psychology assessment;
>
> ■ rating scales and information from schools;
>
> ■ reports from other professionals.

Focus of the questions in the family interview

■ the child's early development;

■ the pregnancy history;

■ speech development;

■ when normal developmental milestones were reached;

■ other illnesses that may be relevant;

■ the child's strengths and positive attributes;

■ behavioural difficulties;

■ educational and learning problems;

■ organisational skills;

■ coordination problems;

- handwriting problems;
- social interaction skills.

For older children

- substance abuse; and
- antisocial tendencies.

The family interview should also assess the relationship between the child and the parents, and consider the sometimes different perceptions of the two parents, or the parents and the school (see 'Information from schools' below). It should also investigate the possibility of other family members, in particular the parents, having ADHD.

Medical examination

The child should have a general and neurological examination. Pulse and blood pressure should be measured and height and weight recorded. An assessment should be made of whether there is any evidence of an underlying syndrome, or any unusual birthmarks that occasionally indicate neurological diagnoses such as neurofibromatosis. Coordination, vision and hearing should all be checked.

Educational psychology assessment

An educational psychology assessment, as part of the comprehensive assessment, provides very important information. Not only does it give the psychologist a chance to observe the child's concentration, impulsiveness, sociability, etc. in an educational setting, but it also provides a framework of current educational ability and potential. However, in many clinics a brief cognitive assessment is done and provided the observer has understanding, not only of specific learning difficulties but also of ADHD, that the child is carefully observed during the assessment, and an idea of overall cognitive ability as well as specific learning difficulties can be obtained, this can be a useful alternative.

As a child's intelligence affects the way in which ADHD presents, it is important to know whether the child is of low, average or high intelligence. For example, a child of high intelligence and potentially high ability may well be perceived as an average student in class – concentration or behavioural problems meaning the child underachieves. It is often easier for teachers to become aware of under-achievement in a child of average intelligence who achieves towards the bottom of the class. When a child is extremely bright and still achieving only average in class, this underachievement is not always so obvious.

Quantitative EEG

Many clinics, including our own, increasingly frequently do a QEEG as part of the assessment process. Such investigations are helpful in confirming the associated brain dysfunction that occurs in ADHD; they enable a formal test that shows brain dysfunction to be done, so that the diagnosis is not just a clinical one as has always been the case in the past. Its use has been likened by some authors to taking the temperature in a child who has a fever and who is unwell as a means of proving that

TEACHER BEHAVIOUR EVALUATION SCALE

Learning Assessment & Neurocare Centre

48–50 Springfield Road

Horsham, West Sussex, RH12 2PD

Tel: 01403 240002 Fax: 01403 260900

Name:_____

Date of Birth:_____ Date:_____

School:_____

Grade/Yr:_____ Teacher:_____

Subject:_____(if applicable)

It would be helpful if you could collate the responses of

a number of teachers, if appropriate.

Each rating should be considered in the context of what is appropriate for the age of the child you are rating and

reflect his/her behaviour.

Please indicate the number of weeks or months you have observed the behaviours: _____

Have you observed the child at differing times of the day and is there a different response?_____

Morning _____   Lunchtime_____   Afternoon_____

Frequency Code: 0 = Never 1 = Occasionally 2 = Often 3 = Very Often

1.	Fails to give attention to details or makes careless mistakes in schoolwork	0	1	2	3	
2.	Has difficulty sustaining attention in tasks or activities perceived as not particularly interesting	0	1	2	3	
3.	Does not listen when spoken to directly	0	1	2	3	
4.	Does not follow through on instructions and fails to finish schoolwork *(not due to oppositional behaviour or failure to understand)*	0	1	2	3	
5.	Has difficulty organising tasks or activities	0	1	2	3	
6.	Avoids, dislikes, or is reluctant to engage in tasks that require sustained mental effort	0	1	2	3	
7.	Loses things necessary for tasks or activities (school assignments, pencils or books)	0	1	2	3	
8.	Is easily distracted by extraneous stimuli	0	1	2	3	
9.	Is forgetful in daily activities	0	1	2	3	
10.	Fidgets with hands or feet or squirms in seat	0	1	2	3	
11.	Leaves seat in classroom or in other situations in which remaining seated is expected	0	1	2	3	
12.	Runs about or climbs excessively in situations in which remaining seated is expected	0	1	2	3	
13.	Has difficulty playing or engaging in leisure activities quietly	0	1	2	3	

Figure 3.1 A typical teacher feedback form as used at our centre

14.	Is 'on the go' or often acts as if 'motor driven'	0	1	2	3	
15.	Talks excessively	0	1	2	3	
16.	Blurts out answers before questions have been completed	0	1	2	3	
17.	Has difficulty waiting in line	0	1	2	3	
18.	Interrupts or intrudes on others (e.g., butts into conversations or games)	0	1	2	3	
19.	Loses temper	0	1	2	3	
20.	Actively defies or refuses to comply with adults' requests or rules	0	1	2	3	
21.	Is angry or resentful	0	1	2	3	
22.	Is spiteful and vindictive	0	1	2	3	
23.	Bullies, threatens, or intimidates others	0	1	2	3	
24.	Initiates physical fights	0	1	2	3	
25.	Lies to obtain goods for favours or to avoid obligations (i.e. 'cons' others)	0	1	2	3	
26.	Is physically cruel to people	0	1	2	3	
27.	Has stolen items of non-trivial value	0	1	2	3	
28.	Deliberately destroys others' property	0	1	2	3	
29.	Is fearful, anxious, or worried	0	1	2	3	
30.	Is self-conscious or easily embarrassed	0	1	2	3	
31.	Is afraid to try new things for fear of making mistakes	0	1	2	3	
32.	Feels worthless or inferior	0	1	2	3	
33.	Blames self for problems, feels guilty	0	1	2	3	
34.	Feels lonely, unwanted, or unloved; complains that 'no one loves him/her'	0	1	2	3	
35.	Is sad, unhappy, or depressed	0	1	2	3	

ACADEMIC PERFORMANCE

	Problematic		Average	Above average		
Reading	1	2	3	4	5	
Mathematics	1	2	3	4	5	
Written expression	1	2	3	4	5	
Homework completion	1	2	3	4	5	

Figure 3.1 *continued*

CLASSROOM BEHAVIOUR

	Problematic		Average	No difficulties		
Relationship with peers	1	2	3	4	5	
Following directions/rules	1	2	3	4	5	
Disrupting class	1	2	3	4	5	
Assignment completion	1	2	3	4	5	
Organisational skills	1	2	3	4	5	

Please include any observations you feel are pertinent:

Figure 3.1 *continued*

something is wrong with the child. Such tests are helpful but are not essential in the diagnosis.

Rating scales and information from schools

There are a number of questionnaires, including the widely used Achenbach and Connors rating scales, that allow teachers and parents to rate children's behaviour, concentration, social skills and mood swings, and assist in the accurate evaluation of ADHD. However, rating scale test scores must be used in conjunction with other clinical information in an assessment, and are insufficient for a diagnosis on their own. The specialist clinic should provide such rating scales to the school as part of its comprehensive assessment.

For an accurate diagnosis, the clinician will need information from all those who have been involved with the child on a long-term basis. Clearly, the school and teachers have a prime role here. Many symptoms will show most readily in the school environment, especially if there have been difficulties with excessive hyperactivity and impulsivity.

Information from earlier school reports is crucial. Teachers may view a child (who is, in reality, predominantly inattentive) as 'not trying hard enough' or 'being too lazy' and 'if only he would concentrate and try harder he would do well'. Or the child may be seen as 'just naughty' when, in fact, this is due to verbal or physical impulsiveness or hyperactivity.

For many children, going to school each day is an act of courage, as the ongoing sense of impotence, despair and frustration because of continued academic and social underachievement, in a downward spiral, is frequently unappreciated.

Reports from other professionals

Teachers' comments on a child with ADHD:
'Bright, interesting and motivated on a one-to-one level and able to concentrate well, retain information and apply it at a later date. Conversely, in class or any small group, the reverse is true to a quite uncommon degree. He is unable to focus upon or follow through any task. All minor movements on the periphery of his field of vision, and distractions and minor comments from others, break his concentration; he becomes listless, unmotivated and abstracted. He is not hyperactive or undisciplined, he simply "absents himself".'

When there are speech and language or coordination problems it may be appropriate to involve specific professionals, such as speech and language or occupational therapists. However, this is often more helpful after the core ADHD symptoms have been treated, when these problems may have partially improved. A speech and language assessment should assess not only articulation but also possible, often subtle, language difficulties, as well as clarity, sequencing and hesitations.

What happens next?

A great deal of care should be taken with the assessment and evaluation, and relevant information shared with the parents and, if old enough, the child. In this way a template of the child's diagnosis and associated strengths and difficulties is developed. This makes later management much more effective and increases the chance of the child's cooperation with treatment. If the child does not have ADHD, the other problems need to be identified and managed appropriately.

The ADHD diagnosis may partially answer many of the unresolved questions about a child's behaviour and life difficulties and can be seen as a springboard from which to go forward. It is generally not a panacea or a 'quick fix'.

A written report of the assessment should be sent to the family GP and to the parents. The report should include a summary of the history and assessment, as well as a management plan, outlined and audited by the clinic. Management strategies should be discussed, and if medication is to be used, arrangements should be made for who will prescribe and whether or not a shared care agreement would be appropriate. The school should also be sent a separate letter outlining the assessment and information regarding implementation of strategies. It is also helpful to include general information on ADHD for the school to use; see information on ADHD and suggested educational strategies in Chapter 4.

For more on management of ADD, see Chapter 4.

Consequences of under-diagnosis of ADHD

ADHD is a very under-diagnosed cause of children's emotional, educational and general health difficulties; it is a hidden handicap, rather than an obvious physical abnormality and is often inappropriately viewed as a wilful problem of self-control rather than as a disability. The all-too-frequent advice to wait a little longer for the child to outgrow the problem is usually incorrect. On the contrary, the problem frequently gets worse, especially at puberty when the complications of excessive oppositionality, Conduct Disorder and associated antisocial activity may occur. Some children outgrow their problems, but many continue with them into adulthood.

Blaming a child's behaviour on poor parenting

There is no evidence to support the commonly held belief that poor parenting is responsible for all problem behaviour in children. Blaming the parents, who have often struggled for years with little support or understanding, aggravates an already stressful situation, destroys parental morale and delays diagnosis.

Since there is a genetic component to ADHD, one or both parents may have the condition. They often give a history of long-standing underachievement, low self-esteem and relationship problems, as well as risk-taking behaviour. In a lower socioeconomic situation it can be particularly hard to differentiate between the effects of the environment and the symptoms of ADHD.

Inadequate parenting can lead to relationship stress, depression and other difficulties, which may aggravate ADHD rather than being the prime cause of the condition. However, family dysfunction often occurs as a result of the severe stress caused by living with ADHD. Many of the children seen at ADHD clinics have previously had their problems attributed to poor parenting and have generally failed to respond to behavioural management only.

Progression of ADHD

Many children and parents attending ADHD clinics find that their stories and anguish are understood for the first time. Parents then realise their child has a medical condition that may have been overlooked in the past and that the frustration caused by the child's downward decline over the years could have been averted. They tend to become re-motivated in supporting their child once a positive direction is identified.

Many parents feel that they have either lost the child they once knew, as the symptoms have progressed, or have never had any positive experiences or relationship with the child. They comment that the child with a bright, bubbly personality and good relationships was gradually lost once school started and much of the seeming ability was replaced by underachievement and loss of self-confidence. They are no longer able to communicate with their child in the same way as they once could and feel frustrated and uncertain as to why these difficulties are occurring.

Inappropriate school provision

In the past, children in special schools for children with emotional and behavioural difficulty (EBD) may have had untreated ADHD. One study showed that 40% of a residential EBD population were still severely hyperactive, and that 75% of the children had either Conduct Disorder or emotional disorder.

Previous child abuse or other environmental difficulties do not necessarily mean that the child might also have associated ADHD. For any child expelled or placed in special schooling provision, ADHD should be considered a possibility. If overlooked, it can continue to cause secondary educational and behavioural problems for the child and the family and require scarce public funds that could otherwise be directed elsewhere.

Managing children with ADHD

Following thorough assessment (see Chapter 3) a management plan should be devised for each child, using the most appropriate combination from a wide range of evidence-based strategies. To be successful it will require the cooperation of all involved, including teachers, parents and the wider family, as well as other professionals as necessary.

> Some professionals and non-professionals alike may see the diagnosis of ADHD as a soft option. However, ADHD should not be used as an excuse – rather as an explanation. Everybody is responsible for their own behaviour, but ADHD treatment will help the child to function to his/her potential, and function more appropriately.

Possible management options

- Educational strategies
- Behavioural strategies
- Psychological or psychiatric strategies
- Neurofeedback
- Medication
- Counselling/coaching
- Alternative therapies
- Changes to diet.

Educational strategies

These are discussed in more detail in the following chapters. Some professionals and non-professionals alike may see the diagnosis of ADHD as a 'soft option'. However, ADHD should not be used as an excuse – rather as an explanation. Everybody is responsible for their own behaviour, but ADHD treatment will help the child to function to his or her potential, and function more appropriately. Educational strategies are always important, whether or not medication is also used. However, their successful implementation requires the teacher to have an understanding of the basis of ADHD and the complications involved for the individual child. Such strategies are aimed at minimising the impact of poor concentration, impulsive and overactive difficulties on the child and the classroom, and also helping with any complications that are present.

The diagnosis of ADHD is not an excuse but rather it is an explanation and it paves the way for subtle rethinking about the approach to the child. It enables a 'disability perspective' to be taken, for it to be recognised that the persistent disruptiveness, loss of concentration and daydreaming is not necessarily within the child's volition and that many children with ADHD have the ability to switch

For more on educational strategies, see Chapter 6.

on, almost with an adrenaline buzz, to things that are interesting but have great difficulty with the mundane. It is important that the various strategies put in place for the child must come from an understanding of ADHD, rather than just from the list of things that are generally found useful.

Behavourial strategies

At home, behavioural interventions include house rules, daily charts, time out, points and token systems, and contracts/negotiations with adolescents. A key strategy is giving appropriate commands; in order to gain the child's attention a command should be given as a command rather than a question; it should be specific and brief, and the consequences of not following it through should be indicated.

In the classroom, similar behavioural strategies are appropriate as discussed in the following chapters. There need to be basic classroom rules, together with structure and organisation. Daily report cards are a particularly good example of effective management, as is a token reward system so that rewards can be earned by good behaviour or by completing academic work.

Psychological or psychiatric strategies

These can be helpful with social skills interventions, improving self-esteem and where there are specific issues around family dysfunction and other environmental problems. Focusing on improving social behavioural competencies, decreasing aggression, improving compliance and gaining closer friendships and relationships can be very helpful. However, traditional psychoanalysis can be counterproductive or even destructive, as it frequently misinterprets ADHD symptoms. For example, the forgetfulness of ADHD may be interpreted as being negative or aggressive in a relationship, and impulsiveness may be interpreted as wilfully disobedient behaviour.

Neurofeedback

There is increasing evidence that neurofeedback – a brain-training programme – can be useful in many children with ADHD. There is now an evidence base that attests to its effectiveness in about three-quarters of the children treated. It has been shown that with regular brain training sessions, which can be done at home, brain wave patterns can be normalised in a high percentage of children with ADHD, and that clinical improvement can be long-lasting.

Medication

The medical management of ADHD is described in more detail later in this chapter. Medication and educational/behavioural strategies have a proven evidence base in the management of ADHD. Thus, if educational, behavioural and psychological strategies in themselves do not improve the situation, and the child has significant ongoing problems, other options, including medication, should be considered. While the core symptoms of **inattentiveness**, **impulsiveness** and **hyperactivity** may be helped by such strategies alone, if the child remains unfocused or excessively impulsive, there is little point in attempting complex teaching or behavioural strategies without the concomitant use of medication to provide a window of opportunity. The aim of medication should be not only to improve the

ADHD problems, but also to improve, as much as possible, the symptoms and to enable the possibility of a more fulfilling life.

In most cases an initial improvement is seen following diagnosis and a management plan, although after the early positive treatment response there is usually a realisation that, while the problems are to some degree improving, they will not necessarily cease. The use of medication and other strategies should be monitored, and regular clinical review is essential. Once medication has stabilised the core ADHD symptoms, there generally is a flow-on improvement to many of the other complicating factors. Reassessment after a few months of treatment is necessary to establish what residual problems are present and how best they might be addressed.

Counselling

In some cases this can be helpful in dealing with secondary problems associated with ADHD, such as low self-esteem and demotivation, by helping the child to recognise his or her islets of competence and capabilities, and to think more positively.

Family counselling may be appropriate when there is a significant degree of family dysfunction that has not improved with the treatment of the child's or adult's ADHD. Such counselling should allow for the possibility of one or both parents having unrecognised ADHD.

Coach/mentor

A coach or mentor needs to be a person who believes in the child with ADHD, has some understanding of the condition, and is able to meet either in person or by phone on a regular, at least weekly, basis to encourage and to help with planning and progress generally.

Because children with ADHD tend very much to think in the 'here and now' and not plan ahead, one of the key roles of the coach is to structure, think ahead, organise and foreshadow forthcoming events, and to develop strategies for the child to remember things like PE kit and directions for football games, etc.

The coach can also be very helpful in reminding, encouraging and helping the child stay focused and on task.

During 'down' periods, encouragement can be very useful and help can be given in avoiding procrastination, providing help with organisation and trying to minimise negative, destructive thinking. All this helps encourage the child's self-esteem and promotes social skills.

We would suggest a regular, at least weekly, meeting at a regular time slot, for between 15 and 30 minutes. There needs to be an agenda and this is often best done with the use of a notebook where items discussed are noted, and these can then be reviewed at the forthcoming meeting. The previous week needs to be looked at and analysed as to where problems occurred, what might have been done to help, and generally encouragement given. The next week is then planned ahead, potential pitfalls identified, and as much praise and support and planning done as possible.

This can thus have a 'stepping stone' effect; it can be very useful as a non-medical strategy for ADHD, and is very effective in promoting self-esteem, and organisational and social skills.

Alternative therapies

Although alternative therapies are frequently trialled by parents of children with ADHD, the evidence that they are effective in managing the core symptoms is sparse at best, though they can sometimes be helpful in decreasing some of the associated factors such as hypersensitivity. Nevertheless, the misinformation that has surrounded the use of medication for ADHD means that many people try alternative therapies initially.

Changes to diet

Evidence of the benefit of dietary modification is minimal, but some parents feel that their child's hyperactivity is helped somewhat by dietary change. For young children in particular, avoidance of some foods may reduce the child's high energy levels, but not the impulsiveness or poor concentration. Anecdotal feedback suggests that diets free of colourings, preservatives and amines are likely to be the most helpful: E numbers 100–50 and preservatives 200–97 should be avoided. However, long-term studies have not shown that dietary manipulation improves the core ADHD symptoms.

Dietary supplements have also been trialled, either as megavitamins or various fish oil-based preparations. Although anecdotal evidence may suggest an improvement in core ADHD symptoms, this is not backed up by scientific data. Studies of mineral and vitamin deficiencies have shown an improvement in blood levels with treatment, but no improvement in the core ADHD symptoms.

Certainly the author's clinical experience is that very few children's ADHD is effectively helped by these therapies, although at times they can provide a more global improvement in well-being and in reducing irritability.

Further details of medication management of ADHD

> Medication improves ADHD symptoms in 80–95% of cases.

Medication is not necessary in all cases of ADHD. However, there is strong evidence that the use of medication, combined with other strategies at an earlier stage, when there are generally fewer complications, is a more effective approach than using other strategies alone. If medication is not considered as part of the management strategy in a person with significant untreated ADHD, the condition will usually progress with a poor prognosis.

When used in conjunction with other strategies, the correct use of medication is one of the most effective forms of therapy in ADHD. Experienced ADHD clinics report an improvement in symptoms in 80–95% of cases. This is substantiated by reports from parents, children and schools that there are continuing improvements which outweigh any side-effects or other disadvantages.

The report of the National Institute of Clinical Excellence in 2008 confirmed that educational and behavioural strategies, as well as medication, were the evidence-based approaches that should be taken for the management of ADHD.

Risks and benefits

The use of any medication for any medical condition has both risks and benefits, and the treatment of ADHD is no exception. However, it is important that side-effects are viewed in perspective and not overemphasised inappropriately, as has tended to be the case previously. Side-effects should be noted as either short or long-term, and should be balanced against the likely improvement in symptoms.

By considering what is likely to happen to the child or adolescent if untreated, a risk assessment of treating or not treating can be made. If medication for ADHD is suggested, there is always an initial trial, to ensure positive effects with minimal or no side-effects, before continuation. Medications for ADHD have been used since the 1950s. Indeed, medications such as Benzedrine were first used for Minimal Brain Dysfunction (earlier terminology for ADHD) in 1937.

Since the 1990s ADHD has been one of the most written-about childhood conditions. There are several hundred well-researched studies on the use of medication for the condition, as well as thousands of general articles. There has been an explosion of research and a general increase in clinical practice in recent years. One study looked at a group of more than 600 children with ADHD and found that in treatment of core ADHD symptoms there was little benefit in adding psychosocial strategies to a finely tuned medication approach. However, the addition of psychosocial strategies improved other aspects of a child's management, such as self-esteem and social skills. Behavioural strategies alone were also quite significant for these factors, whereas the use of medication in a poorly monitored setting was not particularly effective.

In addition to this study, an update on the NICE guidelines has recently been published which guides practitioners in the management of children with ADHD (NICE 2008).

For more on side-effects, see pages 55–57.

Who decides?

Parents generally seek professional help after many years of concern about their child, during which they have tried to cope and have used a wide range of strategies unsuccessfully. They have often been to many different professionals for advice, to no avail. Once ADHD is diagnosed, they usually wish to explore all the available options and receive effective help.

Medication should not be prescribed until there has been a thorough assessment and diagnosis. The possible need for medication must be discussed with the family as part of developing a treatment plan. It is for the parents and the child, if old enough, to decide on whether or not to use medication, following informed discussion with their medical adviser.

It is vital that the school is informed of any decision to treat ADHD with medication. Any medication trial must involve the school so that they can support the child and the parents.

Aim of medication

The aim of medication for ADHD is initially to control the core symptoms and, hopefully, to have a flow-on effect to as many of the coexisting difficulties as possible. In the educational setting it aims to make the child more available for the teaching provided.

The medications prescribed are thought to work by correcting deficiencies in the brain's chemistry on a daily basis for the duration of each dosage. Medication for ADHD cannot be compared with giving a course of antibiotics and expecting a cure. Some individuals may require medication indefinitely, depending on the severity of the condition. Others may require medication only for a shorter period and, with the stabilisation of the situation and the more effective use of educational or behavioural strategies, coupled with an improvement in self-esteem, medication may not be needed for the long term. However, it has been shown that most children diagnosed with ADHD will benefit from the use of medication at least through their school years. Because so many children with ADHD have the ability to switch on and concentrate on interesting subjects, once they get through the initial school years into A-levels, university or careers that they find more interesting, the need for medication can lessen or disappear altogether.

The individual is monitored regularly, the benefits and possible side-effects of the treatment evaluated and the prescription altered if necessary. Giving medication for ADHD can be compared to giving insulin for diabetes or bronchodilators for asthma.

Most of the medications prescribed for ADHD are types of psycho-stimulant. It may seem contradictory to use psycho-stimulants in an already hyperactive child, but they correct the abnormal function in the areas of the brain that are responsible for concentration and impulse control, either by stimulating or inhibiting. The medications used appear to allow the brain's neurotransmitter chemicals, dopamine and noradrenaline, to work more effectively at the synapses, or nerve endings, thereby enabling actions and thought processes to take place smoothly, without being blocked and without digression and side-tracking. This gives the child 'brakes' so that inappropriate activities do not happen so often, and concentration is improved.

Research indicates that problems in dopamine neurotransmission may be responsible for most ADHD core symptoms, although other transmitters have been implicated. There are probably many different neurotransmitter sites and abnormalities involved, accounting for the wide range of expression and differences of response of children with ADHD.

Specific medications used to treat ADHD

In the UK there are three main medication groups used to treat ADHD core symptoms; these are methylphenidate (Equasym, Medikinet XL, Concerta XL), amphetamine based preparations (Dexedrine, Adderall XR) and atomoxetine (Strattera). These medications are internationally recognised as being indicated for use in ADHD when other non-medical strategies have failed.

Most practitioners have tended to start children on methylphenidate preparations in the first instance. The choice of preparation depends on the child's age, educational situation and personal preferences. The longer-acting preparations such as Concerta XL, Medikinet XL and Equasym XL are being used.

Methylphenidate (MPH) is chemically not an amphetamine, which means it is very similar to adrenalin and medications such as bronchodilator asthma puffers. Published studies show no evidence of tolerance or addiction and this confirms clinical practice. Dexedrine (dexamphetamine) is an amphetamine, as its name suggests. However, it, like MPH, shows no evidence of tolerance or addiction when used in the small dose prescribed for ADHD.

Methylphenidate
Traditionally, Methylphenidate has been the most commonly used medication. Until recently it was available only in short-acting preparations, such as Ritalin. A number of preparations have become available in more recent years, such as Concerta XL and modified release Equasym XL and Medikinet XL, which are all

based on methylphenidate but have different delivery systems. They generally last through the school day, between 6 hours and 12 hours, and obviate the need for a child to have a lunchtime dose of medication. This has many advantages within the school setting.

Exactly which preparation is best for an individual child needs to be carefully ascertained. Slow Release Ritalin generally lasts about twice the duration of ordinary Ritalin, i.e. 6–8 hours. Concerta XL, which is the ultra-long-acting methylphenidate preparation, lasts for 10–12 hours in most cases and Equasym XL and Medikinet XL both last about nine hours.

Amphetamine based preparations

Dexedrine has also long been used internationally in the management of children with ADHD. This is a short-acting preparation. There is a group of children with ADHD who either respond better to Dexedrine than methylphenidate or experience fewer side-effects with it. However, it is available as only a short-acting preparation. Adderall XR is similar, but at present it is available only on private prescription. The Dexedrine side-effect profile is similar to that of methylphenidate, but it varies from child to child. In some children Dexedrine will last slightly longer than methylphenidate.

Atomoxetine

The more recent introduction of atomoxetine (Strattera) has added a further option for medical management. Strattera is classified as a non-stimulant and is becoming increasingly popular in the management of children with ADHD. It is long-acting and lasts through the school day, generally for 24 hours. It is particularly effective for behavioural problems at the start and end of the day. Studies have shown a reasonable response to core ADHD symptoms. The side-effects are similar, the main ones being initial lethargy or drowsiness, nausea, headache or abdominal pain. Generally, it is well tolerated and it is not abusable.

Additional medications

The use of additional medications may be considered in children with complex ADHD once the core ADHD is stabilised with the use of the medications described above. They are often critical to obtaining satisfactory management of children with multiple combinations of difficulties such as depression, severe mood instability or anxiety.

Dosage

When the dosage is correctly prescribed and fine-tuned, medication should not sedate the child: rather it should enable normal brain function. Response to medication is very individual, and in some cases, even with careful dosage and timing adjustments, may not be helpful. Some children have an immediate response but, in other cases, response is slower and needs much more fine-tuning. Sometimes a second medication is necessary.

The choice of medication varies depending on the clinical situation. However, as far as possible, the child should be prescribed a longer-acting preparation, either initially or once control is established. In practice, this means using either Concerta XL or Slow Release Ritalin, or Strattera. It may take days or even weeks to determine the correct dosage. Once the correct dosage has been found, medication should help the core ADHD symptoms within about 20 to 30 minutes and usually an improvement in concentration and distractibility is seen. Some of the 'flow-on' effects, such as improving self-esteem and social skills and the lessening of oppositionality, may take weeks or even months to become more apparent. Once improvement is established, appropriate behavioural and educational strategies can be tailored to the child's needs. The lowest dose of stimulant that achieves the optimum result should then be maintained.

In the UK, short-acting Ritalin is available in 10 mg tablets, and Equasym in 5 mg, 10 mg and 20 mg tablets. Dexedrine is available in only 5 mg tablets that can be cut into halves or quarters if appropriate. Short-acting tablets can be crushed and/or inserted into chocolate or banana, dissolved in warm water or given with food. Treatment can be more difficult to initiate in cases where there is severe oppositionality. Equasym XL, another methylphenidate preparation, comes as sprinkles which can be spread on food.

Once the individual's optimum dose and timing is established, the dose usually stays roughly the same over the years, although with age and puberty there is sometimes an increase in dosage. Further fine-tuning or adjustment may be necessary at entry to senior school, with longer school days, more homework, etc.

> Medication should be seen as putting a floor into the situation, treating the core ADHD symptoms and allowing difficulties to improve gradually.

Deciding whether or not to medicate

It is important when deciding whether or not to undertake a trial on medication that parents understand there has been considerable myth and misinformation in both the popular and educational press regarding the use of such medications. A common misconception for teachers, is that if a child can concentrate on interesting subjects or on computers, he or she should be able to concentrate on anything else. While most children will concentrate better if they are interested, children with ADHD are simply unable to concentrate on less interesting topics. The inability to concentrate can appear to be viewed as a rather weak difficulty and something that could improve if the child tried harder. This has often been over-exaggerated in the press with the assumption that the ADHD concept is pathologising normal childhood behaviour. In fact, nothing could be further from the truth.

Sometimes more side-effects occur than should have been the case because of the lack of ability to fine-tune medical management. Side-effects must always be put in context and can be minimised with good collaboration between teachers and the medical profession. The use of the longer-acting preparations has also helped to lessen side-effects and means that children no longer have to queue up at lunchtime for medication and run the risk of being teased.

Getting the best results from medication

Fine-tuning of dosage and timing is essential to successful management. With the short-acting medication it is important that dosage and timing allow continuous coverage during the day. Some children seem to be able to tell when the medication starts to work or to wear off, but others do not notice and are aware of an improvement only because of the comments of those around them.

Mornings can be a particularly difficult time of the day for many children with ADHD, as the medication from the previous evening has worn off. This can be minimised by giving a small dose of medication on waking, followed by the main dose as the child leaves for school.

Doses can be safely overlapped in order to avoid periods in the day when the child is unmedicated, where some children become more hyperactive as the medication wears off (see pages 55–57).

The doctor should give parents clear, concise written instructions and limits of medication dosage to work within. It is generally appropriate for parents to make medication changes within these guidelines, following specific guidance from their medical consultant. Advice should be sought if side-effects persist or if there are problems in dosage adjustment. Most side-effects are transient and can be aggravated by too rapid an increase in dose or too high a dose. There may also be other problems related to timing or short duration of the medication.

If the expected response is not obtained, the dosage may be too low or the timing may be wrong, or it may be that medication is not suitable for the child and alternatives will need to be considered. It may be that, in fact, the core ADHD symptoms – concentration, impulsiveness and hyperactivity – have been improved, but that the residual difficulties lie with coexisting problems, such as oppositionality or obsessions. If a child refuses to swallow tablets because of oppositionality, this is then sometimes treated first so that the child or adolescent is more amenable to the overall concept of medical treatment. The use of longer-acting preparations has tended to lessen many of the issues mentioned above. However, the longer-acting preparations may still need to be combined with some shorter-acting medication to obtain the optimal result. The dose of such medications varies widely. Children with predominantly inattentive ADHD tend to need lower doses than those with hyperactivity.

Few children with ADHD now need to take some of their medication at school with the use of longer-acting medications. The attitude of the staff and whether or not they are supportive of the use of medication, with other strategies, can be extremely important. The child needs to be able to take medication without being teased, bullied or having attention drawn to it. Rather than saying 'Johnny, it's time for your tablet', discreetly drawing the child aside or having a set routine that does not draw too much attention to him or her is far preferable. Some children find the use of an alarm-watch – possibly one that vibrates and that can be set for a number of times – or even a bleeper useful. However, because ADHD children tend to lose things, many children also lose their watches or forget the alarm has gone off.

Side-effects of medication

The medications used to treat ADHD may have possible side-effects, as with any medication for any condition. These are rare and mainly short-term, occurring in 10–20% of children.

> The most common side-effects are described on pages 55–57.

If mild side-effects occur, medication is usually continued as the problems will generally resolve themselves. If side-effects are more significant, the physician may recommend reducing or stopping the medication. Teachers should inform parents of any side-effects that they observe, particularly if the child appears subdued midmorning or if there is any rebound or wearing-off effect in the late morning.

Stimulant medications for ADHD are controlled medications. The information supplied with the tablets should be read carefully. Medication must be kept in a safe place and the amount of medication used must be carefully controlled.

There is no evidence that the medication is addictive at the dosage used to treat ADHD. Once a dose has worn off, children revert to their previous difficult behaviour or poor concentration, in the same way as an asthmatic starts wheezing once the bronchodilator has worn off. Rather than craving their medication, children often forget to take their next dose, especially those who have ADHD-associated short-term memory problems.

Most common short-term side-effects

Short-term side-effects may occur just for the duration of the medication or as it wears off. In practice it is the short-term side-effects that are sometimes of concern. In addition to the side-effects listed below, itchy skin, rashes, a feeling of depression, mood change or nausea can occasionally occur.

- **Appetite suppression**. This is probably the most frequent side-effect. It usually diminishes over the first few weeks of medication, but it can persist, though it is rarely severe enough to warrant cessation of medication. There is sometimes some weight loss over the first few months, but this usually adjusts later on. Eating frequent snacks, or eating late in the day or first thing in the morning when medication has worn off, can sometimes help, as can adjusting the timing and dosage of medication. There may have been pre-existing poor appetite, and sometimes the appetite actually improves on medication because the child is able to sit still long enough to have a meal.

- **Abdominal pain/headaches**. These occasionally occur in the first few days of medication, but rarely persist. Often any headaches and abdominal pain that have been secondary to the stress of untreated ADHD improve once treatment is started.

- **Loss of 'sparkle'**. Transient change in personality can occasionally occur. Some children become irritable, weepy and quite angry or agitated, more commonly with Dexedrine. This may occur either while the medication is working or as it wears off. It can be minimised by making slow dosage adjustments, and usually improves with time or with a slight reduction in dosage. If these side-effects persist, the consultant may recommend stopping the medication. Occasionally, medication may cause some particularly bright children to over-focus, particularly if the dosage is a little too high.

- **Sleep difficulties**. Too high a dosage of medication too late in the day can make it difficult to settle the child for sleep. In some children even a very small dosage at midday will affect sleep, while others can take a higher dose with the evening meal and still sleep well. Sleep difficulties are very much an individual problem and modification of dosage may be necessary. Occasionally, Ritalin can actually improve pre-existing sleep problems.

- **Rebound effect**. Some children, especially those who are hyperactive, become even worse as the medication wears off. If rebound irritability occurs, it is important to ensure the doses are overlapping and this may mean a change of timing.

- **Tics**. Involuntary movements or vocal tics occasionally occur with ADHD and, if severe, may be related to Tourette's Syndrome. Although it is often thought that Ritalin aggravates them, experience shows that it sometimes improves them, and they are not necessarily a contraindication to the use of Ritalin. Sometimes a second medication is necessary to control them. Almost always, if tics have been exacerbated by medication, they ease once the stimulant is ceased, but very occasionally they can be persistent. It is unusual for tics to be aggravated if the child does not also have obsessive tendencies.

Long-term side-effects

- **Possible growth suppression**. Very rarely, transient growth suppression in height can occur but this virtually always corrects with puberty.
- There is no evidence of long-term addiction, blood disorders, liver, cardiac or kidney malfunctions, or other long-term problems with the use of the medications prescribed for ADHD.

What to expect from medical management

Medication, in conjunction with other strategies, can produce marked change. For the first few months there is usually a very rapid improvement in the core symptoms and often in some of the other features. Generally, a chronic, intransigent situation is significantly improved so that a window of opportunity can be created for the more effective use of educational, behavioural and other strategies. The aim of medication is to make the child more available for learning so that other non-medical strategies can be more effective.

The relief that parents and teachers, let alone the child, often feel initially when they realise that something can be done is usually replaced by the realisation, after a few months, that the problem will be ongoing, and even with treatment it may possibly be long-term. A miraculous transformation should not be expected, as there are often many difficulties to improve, which in many cases can take a long time. Ongoing monitoring and cooperation between school, parents and physician is essential.

> **Typical school report**
> 'There has been a considerable metamorphosis of Adam this term. He has displayed interest and enthusiasm towards the subject. Some of his contributions during discussions have exposed a hitherto unrecognised knowledge and intuitive understanding of the subject. I can safely say that it is one of the most pleasing experiences of my professional career.'

> 'He is now able to go on school trips.'
>
> 'Whole demeanour is different.'
>
> 'I was choked when he got his first birthday party invitation. He's never had one before.'

Successful medical management should lead to:

1 **Improved concentration, impulsiveness and distractibility**. The purpose of medication is to improve these core symptoms of ADHD. Oppositionality, aggression and hyperactivity may also show improvement once the core ADHD symptoms are managed effectively. Short-term memory usually improves, as does the ability to learn and perform at school. More slowly, there is usually an improvement in self-esteem and socialising ability, in relationships, in learning ability and in mood swings. Being off-task, not listening, impulsiveness and overactivity are decreased.

2 **Improvement in concentration and behaviour in the classroom**. If there are associated specific learning difficulties, progress may be slower. It is

> Approximately 90% of children with ADHD will show a very significant improvement. About 40% of these will have ongoing difficulties because of other coexisting conditions.

often very difficult to assess the severity of associated specific learning difficulties until the ADHD is treated.

3 **Frequent improvement of verbal, emotional and physical impulsiveness**. These symptoms may be difficult to disentangle from symptoms of Oppositional Defiant Disorder, which may also be improved once the core ADHD features are managed effectively. There is generally an improvement in verbal expression and speech clarity. More complicated language difficulties are slower to improve, but may gradually improve with time, once the child is more focused and more socially aware. Medication allows the situation to stabilise and then enables the residual difficulties to be helped in a more effective way.

4 **Maintained improvements if medication is continued**. Once ADHD is treated appropriately the improvements are generally maintained, provided a combination of strategies is used – including medication – and the situation is regularly assessed and the approach modified as needed.

5 **Long-term use of medication**. This will depend on the severity of the medical condition, the age at diagnosis, the number of complications, and other factors. Once the core ADHD is managed effectively, other problems can often be dealt with more easily. Usually the child's self-esteem and social skills also improve. Children on medication should be regularly monitored and reviewed to assess whether the benefits of medication outweigh any other difficulties.

If there is no improvement

If the child does not respond to one medication, then an alternative stimulant should be used. If the core ADHD symptoms are managed effectively, but there is continued depression, obsessions, oppositionality or tics, then a second medication may be necessary.

Occasionally, a child who has been well controlled on a certain dose of medication seems to become less effective in response to another medication. In this situation, changing to the other stimulant, or stopping the medication for a few weeks and then restarting, is the most effective form of management.

Medical management in specific situations

Teenagers

As ADHD is a progressive condition, many teenagers are excessively oppositional and sometimes conduct-disordered, which may make it impossible to initiate medical management because of lack of compliance and excessive oppositionality. If the oppositionality can be modified, psycho-stimulants can then be introduced to improve concentration. Unfortunately, most teenagers resist parental interference at this stage and it is very hard to remind them to take their medication. Diagnosing and then treating an adolescent with ADHD initially in teenage years is like trying to stop a car going at 100 mph rather than at 30 mph – it takes a lot longer. There are usually a number of issues to contend with, but after 12 to 18 months persistent improvement can be seen.

Children under six years of age

The use of stimulants in such children has caused considerable debate and discussion. Methylphenidate is licensed for children who are six years of age and above. There is, however, a wide body of international opinion that attests to the safety and effectiveness of medication when used in children under six where indicated.

Experienced practitioners involved in the care of ADHD children acknowledge that there is a group who need treatment at a younger age and who, in fact, often do much better if this is the case. Some studies show that children who present with the early onset of ADHD may be a more virulent group and that they may more frequently have other coexisiting conditions, such as the early onset of Oppositional Defiant Disorder and/or learning or language difficulties, in addition to their ADHD. Early treatment enables them to access the curriculum more easily, develop appropriate social skills and improve their learning or language difficulties.

Children with ADD

Such children may need to be treated with medication only during the school hours, provided they cope with homework, there are no significant behavioural problems and self-esteem is reasonable. They generally respond very well, and often to very low doses of medication, unless complicated by significant anxiety or depression.

ADHD and Asperger's Syndrome

It is less likely that such children can be treated successfully, although when it can be achieved it can make a great functional difference to the child. When the obsessions and the core ADHD symptoms are treated successfully, this can help the child cope more effectively with the other difficulties. However, more frequent side-effects or complete lack of response are common in this group. Often a low dose of medication, combined with low-dose Fluoxetine Syrup or Clomipramine to help with the obsessions and rituals, can be very helpful.

ADHD with severe Oppositional Defiant Disorder and/or Conduct Disorder, especially of early-onset (Disruptive Behavioural Disorder)

If a child has ongoing oppositionality, impulsiveness and/or Conduct Disorder despite the core symptoms being effectively managed by methylphenidate or dexamphetamine, he or she might benefit from clonidine, which often has the effect of decreasing the intensity and frequency of such difficulties. Originally used in high doses as a medication for high blood pressure, clonidine is also effective in low doses in 60–70% of children with persistent oppositionality. Other medications that may be effective include Sodium Valproate, Carbamazepine, Risperidone.

ADHD with associated anxiety, depression or obsessions

If anxiety, depression or obsessions persist once the core ADHD symptoms have been treated, this may warrant the introduction of a second medication, such as Fluoxetine.

ADHD with coexisting manic depression (bipolar disorder)

The stimulants prescribed for ADHD may aggravate the manic depression. Anticonvulsants such as Carbamazepine or Sodium Valproate may be helpful, as may atypical antipsychotic medications such as Risperidone.

ADHD with tics and/or Tourette's Syndrome

The ADHD symptoms are usually much more of a handicap to the child than are the tics. Studies show that with the use of stimulants, 15% of tics will get worse, 15% will get better and in the remaining 70 per cent there is no change. Clonidine is frequently effective in the management of tics. Other medications that can be used include Pimozide and Sulpiride. Tics should not be treated unless they are significantly interfering with the child's function. Often the tics will wax and wane as part of the condition and may be exacerbated by the amount of stress in the child's life.

ADHD with substance abuse and Conduct Disorder

Although traditionally associated with one another, ADHD and Conduct Disorder have previously been treated only after the substance abuse disorder has been managed appropriately. Now, however, there is increasing clinical experience in treating all conditions at the same time, using family and individual therapy (drug action teams) and support as well as psycho-pharmacological intervention, where appropriate. Treating the ADHD and Conduct Disorder often allows the adolescent or adult to be helped more effectively with their substance abuse management and have less need for substances.

Professionals and services for ADHD

In a school of 1,000 pupils, approximately 10 will have severe ADHD and at least a further 20 will have less severe variants of ADHD.

Because ADHD is such a common condition, with such a wide range of presentations, it impacts on many different professions and service providers. It is therefore essential that all professionals understand the true facts and reality of ADHD in order to help and manage people with ADHD under their care most effectively and to offer more effective services.

Of course, teachers have a special responsibility in the management of children with ADHD. Up to 5% of schoolchildren have the condition, making it one of the most common conditions that teachers will encounter. An awareness of the condition, a non-judgemental approach to its management and the ability to work in a seamless way with other professionals are essential. This particularly applies to special educational needs coordinators (SENCOs) who also need an understanding of the links between ADHD, dyslexia and developmental coordination difficulties.

A number of studies have shown that children in special schools, particularly schools for children with emotional and behavioural difficulties and pupil referral units, have a higher likelihood of having ADHD. Therefore, teachers in these schools need to be particularly aware of the condition, its complexity and how it may be accompanied or even masked by coexisting conditions. There is also a high incidence of ADHD in children who have been excluded from mainstream schools.

Educational psychologists frequently assess children with educational and/or behavioural difficulties. Again, a non-judgemental, well-informed approach to the possibility of a child having ADHD is essential. The British Psychological Guidelines on ADHD, published in 2000, are an important basis.

Among medical practitioners, **GPs** have a key role, not only in initial referral for assessment, but also in continuing prescription of medication, if used, and in providing general support to the family.

A comprehensive assessment to determine whether or not a child has ADHD should be carried out by either a **child psychiatrist** or **community paediatrician**. Both professions have much to add to the diagnosis and management of children with ADHD, but which one is employed depends very much on the availability of local services. Since they are involved with children from birth, **health visitors** are in an excellent position to identify those who have extreme hyperactivity, early oppositionality and severe sleep difficulties. Their liaison with the general practitioner can be very helpful. **School nurses** are also critical in identifying and helping to manage children with ADHD.

Many other therapists may come into contact with children with ADHD. For example, as about one third of children with ADHD have, or have had, a speech and language problem, **speech therapists** are frequently involved. Sometimes it is necessary not only to provide speech and language assistance but also to treat the child's ADHD. **Occupational therapists** have a similar role. In diagnosing a child with developmental coordination disorder or dyspraxia, they must also consider that a child who is also inattentive or hyperactive may have coexisting ADHD.

Children with ADHD, especially where there is the early onset of associated Conduct Disorder, are frequently referred to **social services departments**. ADHD is common in adopted children because of genetic factors. It is also common in children with challenging behaviours. Young parents with ADHD, especially if they also have Conduct Disorder, have higher rates of child abuse and domestic violence.

The group of people with ADHD and associated Conduct Disorder have a much higher chance of being involved with the **criminal justice system**; thus an awareness of ADHD is important for all those involved with the youth justice service, with magistrates, with lawyers and with the judiciary. ADHD may compromise a person's ability to testify and give evidence. Studies show that treating ADHD, as well as including rehabilitation programmes, greatly reduces the risks of reoffending. Involving ADHD and dyslexic strategies in education in prison programmes is also important.

> For more on such studies, see the publications listed under 'Learning difficulties' in Appendix 1.
>
> For more on coexisting conditions, see Chapter 2.

> 'Munchausen's Syndrome by Proxy' may be erroneously diagnosed in parents of children with severe, unrecognised ADHD.

Summary

There are some children with ADHD whose difficulties can take a while to improve, or who are a particular challenge to treat, but there is no doubt that most children who would have ended up with significant problems are greatly helped. Treatment with medication significantly enhances the quality of the child's relationships at home and at school, in time.

The length of time a child will need to be on medication varies. Experience seems to show that children can be greatly helped if they are treated before complications arise, but there are no firm data on this. One of the myths of ADHD is that it disappears by puberty. In reality, by teenage years it is often much worse and is compounded and masked by other difficulties. Hyperactivity has often diminished, but this does not mean there are no other problems. In fact, it is often necessary to treat teenagers, and also adults, as a proportion of people are affected with the condition into adulthood.

Some children outgrow the need for medication during school years and many more discontinue medication when they leave school. Although many of their ADHD symptoms may continue, provided they can get through school with protected self-esteem and reasonable academic and behavioural achievements, in later life they may be able to focus, or indeed over-focus, on things they are really interested in, without necessarily needing to continue medication.

Case studies

The case studies here illustrate a range of problems seen with children with ADHD. They are included to illustrate the descriptions of ADHD given in the earlier chapters of this book, and in particular the management strategies outlined in Chapter 4 and the educational strategies outlined in Chapter 6. Because of the wide range of presentations of children with ADHD, the following case studies may be helpful for teachers in the identification and management of a child with ADHD.

Case studies: ADHD and various symptom patterns

- Glen: moderately severe ADHD, see page 64.
- Leighton: combined ADHD with early-onset ODD and specific learning difficulties, see page 65.
- Chris: hyperactivity, see page 66.
- James: gifted with ADHD, see page 67.

Case studies: ADHD and other conditions requiring further medication

- Alan: combined ADHD plus early-onset ODD and Conduct Disorder, see page 68.
- Mitchell: late diagnosed combined ADHD, ODD, Conduct Disorder, learning difficulties and substance abuse, see page 69.
- Sonia: combined ADHD, Conduct Disorder, anxiety, pregnancy, see page 70.

CASE NOTES	Glen

Moderately severe ADHD

History

Glen's mother had worked for many years in a school for children with emotional and behavioural difficulties. When Glen was 12 years old she realised that ADHD was a common, underlying factor in many such children and she noted that, although Glen was in mainstream school, he was struggling. His concentration was very poor and his school reports repeatedly commented on his obvious ability, but his inability to put his mind to things and take notice of what he was doing. He had never been able to concentrate long enough to read a book and she felt that if he could concentrate he would learn a lot better. He was very disorganised. She said it was a month of hard work trying to tidy up his bedroom, and he had very little routine. He didn't think ahead and he lived for the moment; he often couldn't participate in sports day because he forgot his PE kit and was always losing things. Almost every week she had to buy a new set of pencils and he never had any idea of where he had left things. He had very few friends, was never asked out or invited to parties and his self-esteem was low. With the onset of puberty he was starting to become more and more oppositional. A wide range of educational and behavioural strategies had previously been tried, but without improvement.

Assessment

Glen was of average intelligence, with combined ADHD, and 1–2 years behind in his reading, spelling and maths attainments. There were no other associated specific learning difficulties, some features of mild Oppositional Defiant Disorder, low self-esteem, occasional mild motor tics and some mild obsessional features.

Management

A trial of methylphenidate and associated supported behavioural and educational strategies resulted in a very dramatic initial improvement in his core ADHD symptoms and a subsequent improvement in all his other problems over the ensuing months. He started to develop more lasting friendships, to be asked out more, and his self-esteem improved. In class he was able to concentrate much better, to be better organised and less impulsive, and to achieve his age-appropriate ability. On medication, there were some initial problems with sleeping which gradually improved, and also his tics disappeared.

In the classroom he needed basic educational support strategies with structure – seating him towards the front of the class – and clear rules and organisation. He needed help in getting his homework to and from school and was also helped with the use of a daily report card. He did require special needs support to help him catch up with his delay in reading, maths and spelling, but once he was able to catch up, with the use of medication, this made a great deal of difference to his academic achievement.

Combined ADHD with early-onset ODD and specific learning difficulties

History

Leighton, aged nine, had for two years been at a residential school for children with emotional and behavioural difficulty (EBD), following his exclusion from mainstream school. He had been extremely active from birth, and this continued at preschool. At nursery school he became increasingly angry, defiant and oppositional, and was excluded. His mother commented that as a five-year-old he was virtually running their family life. When he started at mainstream school, his disruption, class clowning and poor concentration continued. He was eventually excluded, following a string of severe emotional outbursts and bullying of other children.

His parents had previously sought professional advice and the behaviour was blamed on his parents' divorce when Leighton was aged two. The parents disputed this as they felt that his mother's subsequent remarriage had led to a continuing very stable relationship, although Leighton had put a great deal of pressure on this. Leighton's mother felt that he was very much like his natural father who had struggled at school and left early, and eventually entered jail.

Assessment

Leighton had very significant functional difficulties with virtually all of the main ADHD criteria, both at home and even at the EBD school, despite the small class size and a great deal of structure. In addition, he had a number of other complicating difficulties including Oppositional Defiant Disorder of early onset, associated specific learning difficulties, poor handwriting and low self-esteem.

Management

1. Because of the severe, complicated and persistent history, Leighton was started on methylphenidate (Ritalin) to treat his core ADHD symptoms. Fine-tuning of dosage and timing was necessary to avoid rebound effects. This resulted in an almost immediate, dramatic improvement in the core symptoms, such that he was able to concentrate. He reacted much less impulsively and became less hyperactive.

2. Over the next few months there was a slower, but very significant, improvement in almost all of his other problems. His oppositional symptoms became much more manageable, his handwriting improved and his self-esteem also improved, though more slowly. He had ongoing specific learning difficulties, but once he was able to concentrate he was able to benefit from the intensive educational support. He became less frustrated and angry.

3. After a further 12 months, he was slowly integrated into mainstream school. He still required the basic educational supportive strategies and needed an ongoing behavioural modification approach with a school–home diary and a daily report card. There was ongoing communication and monitoring with the school, via the school liaison officer, and significant continuous educational support via his Statement of Special Needs.

4. Supportive individual and group counselling helped Leighton cope with his ADHD and with his previous difficulties.

CASE NOTES   Chris

ADHD

History

Chris was a nine-year-old boy who was thoroughly assessed and diagnosed with having ADHD with no other significant complications. He met all of the ADHD criteria and had done so even as a preschooler. His mother had tried a number of dietary manipulations which had reduced his hyperactivity a little, and it had lessened somewhat with time; but he was still very active and was especially verbally impulsive, inattentive and highly distractible. His teachers commented that in the class 'as soon as his hand went up his mouth opened'. Although he was underachieving a little in class he was not receiving extra support. His self-esteem and social skills were causing some moderate difficulties, but there were no other complicating factors apart from poor handwriting. He was of slightly above average intelligence and achieving to just below his chronological age level.

Management

1. Educational strategies were implemented. He sat at the front of the class, the teacher cued him in, gave him brief instructions and tried hard to nurture his self-esteem. He was also supported during the unstructured playtimes, and this helped a little with his social skills, although there were still problems.

2. After a term of observation, as his problems persisted, a trial of medication (methylphenidate) showed a dramatic improvement in all of his core ADHD symptoms, especially his concentration and impulse control. Chris was then able to achieve much more readily, educationally, and although the educational strategies were still necessary, they were able to be implemented less intensively. His self-esteem and social skills subsequently improved and he did well in the end-of-year examinations.

CASE NOTES	James

Gifted with ADHD

History

James had been extremely active in the womb and his parents knew that he was different from a very early age. He had never been a 'real' baby, according to the parenting books, and was always trying to look around or strain his neck towards something. He wasn't particularly cuddly.

He progressed very quickly and did not walk but ran. At age two he developed frequent tantrums, head-banging and cried a great deal. Cutting out food colourings calmed him a little, although he was always 'on the go'. Even now, food colourings aggravate his behavioural difficulties.

He started at nursery at two. There were lots of problems; he was always running around, and the nursery staff had difficulty in controlling him. He was bright and understood things very quickly yet displayed appalling behaviour. When he was three, his verbal comprehension was age five level, and later educational assessment showed a general intelligence ability of about 130.

Starting school, aged four years eight months, brought problems from the first day. He did not settle, he was disruptive, he called out and he seemed to move from one task to another without accomplishing any of them successfully. The teacher noticed his poor concentration and motivation, which contrasted with his very marked academic ability. He had very few friends, was constantly demanding attention, was unwilling to listen, was aggressive to teachers and other students, and was non-conformist. He found sitting still very difficult and was always touching things. However, his teachers noted that there was a loving, affectionate side to him and that he was a lovely character. The ongoing problems meant that he moved school at age five and a half, but the problems resurfaced very quickly. The school thought it was all due to bad behaviour and poor parenting. His educational testings at five and a half were at nine-year-old level. His teacher noted that he had a remarkable ability in explaining concepts and in reading and mathematics, and on a one-to-one basis he showed sound and deep levels of understanding. However, in group activities he would readily become impatient and disruptive, had difficulty in focusing and staying on task and required constant supervision. At times, his behaviour was bizarre and even frightening.

Assessment

His parents became increasingly concerned that something else was wrong and that he would never fulfil his potential. They became aware of ADHD and an educational psychology assessment was done. This showed an IQ score of 148, and thus indicated enormous ability. There was no sign of dyslexia, but his short concentration span and impulsivity were noted, as were his excellent vocabulary, number skills, sentence construction and comprehension.

Management

After thorough assessment and discussion, a diagnosis of ADHD was made and a trial of medication (methylphenidate) was commenced. The response was impressive. His parents and school noticed a transformation and that he was a different child who now wanted to go to school. There was an immediate improvement in all the areas that had been concerning them, and the school said it was like a switch being turned on. There was such a difference in his work that he was able to achieve according to his high ability. His behaviour improved and he was no longer disruptive. Slowly, his self-esteem improved. His grandparents even offered to babysit for him for the first time!

The ongoing educational strategies involved some minor need for educational structure and support in the classroom, and, additionally, an awareness by the school that he was gifted and needed an accelerated programme to maintain his interest.

There were some ongoing social issues, partly because of his giftedness and partly because of his fluctuating self-esteem. These slowly improved with time, but he tended to need structure and support, especially during playtime. The school worked hard on nurturing his self-esteem and providing a supportive schooling environment that made a great deal of difference to him.

Over the next few years he continued to make excellent progress, both academically and socially. He still could have difficulties without structure or support, and at times socially, but the combination of medication, an understanding of ADHD and the correct supportive schooling environment made a great difference to James.

CASE NOTES	Alan

ADHD with early-onset Oppositional Defiant Disorder and Conduct Disorder

History

Alan, age six, came for assessment with his mother and his social worker. He had been extremely active, even *in utero* and certainly from birth. He had been aggressive, oppositional and excessively impulsive from a very early age. The family were very stressed because of severe financial pressure, and the parents were at loggerheads. He was the second eldest of four children, all under eight. Prior to starting school a number of agencies and professionals had seen him. He had been placed on the 'at risk' register because of being hit by his father in a fit of temper after another night of his not sleeping and being persistently disobedient. Alan was struggling at school. His speech development was slow and unclear and he had a stammer.

Assessment

In addition to being severely hyperactive, Alan's teachers also noted that he had a very poor concentration span and was persistently verbally and physically impulsive. The assessment confirmed that he was severely hyperactive, had very poor concentration and was very impulsive. He had the worrying combination of early-onset oppositionality and Conduct Disorder, together with severe learning and language problems. He was placing an enormous amount of stress on an already pressurised family. There was a combination of ADHD and early-onset Oppositional Defiant Disorder, together with learning problems and environmental issues.

Management

1. An initial trial of methylphenidate made him much more aggressive.

2. His prescription was therefore changed to dexamphetamine 5mg tablets, and by slowly adjusting the dosage and timing an improvement in his concentration and a marked reduction in his impulsivity and hyperactivity were obtained. His initial appetite suppression improved.

3. However, his oppositionality persisted, as did his verbal impulsiveness and sleep difficulties. The addition of clonidine in the morning and evening slowly made him less oppositional and his outbursts less frequent. He also slept better.

4. Liaison with and support from the school enabled him to continue in mainstream education with a Statement of Special Educational Needs. Alan needed a great deal of structure and avoidance of distraction, and his school was very supportive. At school, he needed two doses of dexamphetamine during the school day because the medication only lasted two-and-a-half hours and he became more oppositional during the rebound period.

5. Supportive and marital counselling were given through the local guidance services and the parents were also given help with parenting strategies.

6. The family were eventually rehoused two years later.

His parents commented that just having Alan sleeping put less pressure on the family; they were less tired and were able to cope better with some of the difficulties. This, together with a mellowing of his oppositionality and aggressive behaviour, greatly improved the family functioning. With his increased concentration at school he benefited much more from the support offered to him and achieved much more in class.

Mitchell

Late-diagnosed combined ADHD, ODD, Conduct Disorder, learning difficulties and substance abuse

History

At 15 years of age Mitchell had been permanently expelled from school for fighting with other children. He had even been expelled from preschool and playgroup and had been angry, aggressive and oppositional as a toddler. His parents had always felt that he was bright but had never achieved his true potential, whereas the school regarded them as over-anxious, pushy parents. Once he started school he had increasingly become angry and defiant, his self-esteem had lowered and he became demoralised and continued to struggle with relationships.

Even the cat was scared of him, having been often thrown downstairs, chased, hit and had its fur cut off. His parents had to put a lock on the hamsters' cage when he was younger because he would squeeze and torment them. He was constantly destructive at home and in the garden. He was obsessed by flames and matches – once he set fire to the bin in the playground, and on another occasion he set light to some books and almost burned the house down.

At puberty he started to drink heavily and was intermittently involved in drug-taking. He tended to mix with similar types of boys and friendships did not last long. In class, he was disruptive, spoke out of turn, put up his hand without knowing the answer and generally clowned around. His speech was unclear, his concentration was poor and his reports always commented on his poor concentration and easy distractibility. His teachers said, 'He is great at arguing but has zero logic'.

Assessment

He had an average IQ score, but his reading, writing, spelling and mathematics were at age 8–9 levels, suggesting that he had an associated specific learning difficulty. Apart from clearly having ADHD, he also had Oppositional Defiant Disorder, Conduct Disorder, speech and learning problems and intermittent depression.

Management

1. Methylphenidate improved concentration and impulsivity. However, he remained very oppositional.

2. Because of this and because of the sleep problems, after three months clonidine was added. This helped improve oppositionality and sleep and there was a great improvement in his overall well-being.

3. In parallel with this, supportive counselling and coaching were instituted, and he was given help with time management. He found he was no longer dependent on drugs and alcohol.

4. A Statement of Special Educational Needs was processed rapidly, he was placed in a pupil referral unit, and gradually, over six months, reintegrated to mainstream school.

5. He had help in a small group for social skills and gradually he discarded his old group of friends and developed more lasting friendships.

CASE NOTES	Sonia

Combined ADHD, ODD, Conduct Disorder, anxiety and pregnancy

History

Sonia, aged 15, had a long-standing history of hyperactivity. She was adopted at three weeks and was extremely oppositional and antisocial by age eight. She had been expelled from several schools, had frequent difficulties with the youth justice system and had been placed in a pupil referral unit. She also tended to be very anxious, to have phobias and panic attacks and her self-esteem was extremely poor. She experimented with drug-taking, had many undesirable friends and her parents had been extremely concerned, feeling that every strategy had failed, and did not know what to do.

She frequently spent weekends in a social services respite home. There, one of the care workers felt that she might have ADHD and suggested that her parents explore this further.

Assessment

Sonia clearly had ADHD with many complications, including Oppositional Defiant Disorder and Conduct Disorder.

Management

1. A trial of methylphenidate was undertaken and she improved dramatically. However, she remained anxious and oppositional and within three months of starting methylphenidate she became pregnant.

2. Methylphenidate was ceased during the early part of the pregnancy as effects on the foetus are not fully known, and then continued later on. The labour was uneventful and a normal baby girl was born, who is developing well.

3. Sonia copes well with the baby, finds that she very much needs to take her methylphenidate to cope and has been helped by the addition of a low dose of antidepressant because of panic attacks and excessive anxiety. Her teachers had always felt that she was extraordinarily bright and she subsequently went back to college, achieved two As and a B at A-level and is now thinking about entering the legal profession.

What teachers can do

It is easy to underestimate how uncomfortable school can be for a child with ADHD. A child who cannot sit still, cannot remember what has just been said, cannot copy accurately from the board and who finds it difficult to make and keep friends can find school a hostile place. Such a child's wonderful qualities and creativity may get lost in the struggle. Academic underachievement, behavioural problems and socialising difficulties, together with coexisting problems such as specific learning difficulties, depression or anxiety, may further complicate the situation. Children with ADHD have a wide range of difficulties, and no two pupils will be the same; thus there can be a wide range of needs within the classroom.

For some children the main problems are with relative academic achievement, but this may be masked if the child has an above-average IQ. For others the behavioural difficulties are more of a problem – they will push the boundaries, violate classroom rules, call out in class and be increasingly disruptive. For some children, socialising difficulties affect their free time and ability to form friendships. These difficulties may fluctuate, so that the learning difficulties may be more of a problem at some times and the behaviour problems at others. The impulsiveness of ADHD may be expressed both physically and, as a child gets older, more verbally. This impulsiveness frequently impedes effective social interaction.

A comprehensive educational and medical specialist assessment is essential for a diagnosis of ADHD to be made. This assessment will determine whether or not ADHD is present, and also identify any coexisting conditions. The main strategies that have been scientifically evaluated to be effective in children with ADHD are the use of medication and the use of behavioural modification, both in the classroom and in the home. Effective school strategies are always essential in the management of any child with ADHD, whether or not medication is used. It is important for teachers to have a factual understanding of ADHD so that they can implement effective behavioural strategies appropriate to the child.

> The most effective strategies in managing children with ADHD are medication and behavioural modification.

Teachers also need to understand the role of medication as part of the treatment of ADHD. The use of medication should never be seen as an 'either/or' situation. Medication stabilises the situation, improves the concentration span, helps with impulse control and lessens hyperactivity, i.e. treats the core ADHD symptoms, and thus allows educational and behavioural management strategies to be more effective.

The facilities available within the schools in the UK vary quite widely. Some schools run nurture groups that can be helpful in further developing social skills. Other schools run social skills training programmes, and varying other programmes to help reduce aggressive and bullying behaviours. Special education needs coordinators (SENCOs) are increasingly being specifically trained in these neurodevelopmental conditions. School nurses are also a particularly valuable resource, linking in with local child and adolescent mental health services and

> For more on medication, see Chapter 4.

paediatric services. However, the role of the school nurse varies quite considerably. There have been a number of governmental policies in the past decade that have increasingly recognised the importance of ADHD as a significant educational and mental health problem. Other important school-based professionals include educational psychologists, speech and language therapists, behavioural support teams, classroom support assistants, school counsellors, and occupational therapists. In addition, pastoral staff who are particularly able to act as mentors can be very useful. Studies show that these are often teachers who first become aware of the ADHD difficulties and its impact on academic performance and behaviour. A high percentage of parents of children with ADHD have been shown to have discussed their concerns with the child's teacher. Thus teachers are important not only in the initial diagnostic and awareness situation but also in ongoing management. The National Institute of Clinical Excellence guidelines of September 2008 (www.nice.org.uk) was an important benchmark in the increased recognition of the validity and the importance of ADHD as a public and mental health problem. It particularly encourages schools and providers of services to increasingly recognise the importance of social, behavioural and emotional difficulties in the educational system and to recognise, within this group of children, those who may have difficulties such as ADHD. The report encouraged the provision of non-medical approaches in the first instance, but recognised the importance of the additional use of medication in those children who had significant and ongoing difficulties. Whilst specific recommendations were made for medical practitioners, important suggestions were also made for the educational community and for school nurses.

The areas that were of particular importance to educators included:

1. The emphasis that ADHD can be a lifespan condition and is not just a condition of young childhood. A high percentage of children with ADHD continue to have difficulties into late youth and into adulthood.

2. Recognition of the fact that there should be ongoing training not only for medical practitioners but also for teachers, in the symptoms in the school setting that might alert to the possibility of a child having ADHD.

3. That the report encouraged teachers to discuss the possible management strategies and ways forward with the child and with their parents. It suggested that there should be a clear way forward demarcated with ongoing communication with parents.

4. The report also encouraged teacher participation in providing information for the assessment and in ongoing support.

5. The report recognised that transition periods particularly between junior and senior schools could be very difficult for children with ADHD.

Additional classroom support is often necessary. Particularly in senior schools many pupils with ADHD are resistant to this sort of help and often do not recognise that they might benefit from this. Many children with ADHD are poor self monitors and tend to have little insight into their difficulties with problems in monitoring and regulating how they behave. The varying levels of support that are available include initially School Action where minimal levels of support are introduced, then School Action Plus which is where more resources are put in place coming from the school's own budget and where an individual educational plan is done.

For children with significant and ongoing difficulties a statement of special educational needs can be requested. Unfortunately this often involves the parents going to tribunal and there has been considerable debate particularly recently regarding the merits of the current system.

There are a range of specific accommodations that may be helpful for individual pupils. These can include a recording device to take lectures or possibly the use of a scribe during examinations. Other accommodations include computerised technology such as whiteboard and other computer techniques to give students copies of lecture notes to help with mind mapping, with planning, organisation and time management, and in the structure of essays and assignments. Many pupils with ADHD benefit from the accommodation and the extra time for examinations. They may also benefit from being in a quiet room where there are fewer distractions.

Some children with severe associated developmental coordination difficulties may benefit from voice dictation programmes and others benefit from the use of a computer if they are able to touch-type perfectly. It is important that the appropriate specific accommodations be identified for each pupil and if medication is utilised that this be done after the response to medication is assessed. Such strategies must be seen as accommodations and are very appropriate and necessary for these pupils. They should be seen as contributing to the provision of an appropriate level of academic support that is an essential right for children with disabilities such as these. Studies show that such interventions are much less likely to be effective without the additional support of medication in the dose that is required. This runs counter to previous educational ideas in helping those with behavioural and learning difficulties where classroom support only was available. The additional use of medication is a strategy to make the child more available for learning, and thus both physicians and educators need to be able to work together and to be involved in the child's progress.

Common misconceptions about ADHD

Teachers may encounter some of the following misconceptions about ADHD:

- **'If he tried harder to concentrate I am sure he could do it.'** ADHD presents in a number of ways. In the inattentive form there are usually no behavioural problems, but children have relative difficulty in concentrating, especially on more mundane tasks. No matter how hard they try to concentrate, they simply cannot do it. Such children may be seen as 'lazy'.

- **'He can concentrate on computers and other interesting things for hours, but when he tries to do his homework he is up and down all the time.'** There is a common misconception in educational circles that concentration is an 'all or nothing' situation. It has been clearly shown that many children, especially if they are bright, are able to over-focus on subjects which they find interesting, but are just unable to concentrate on other tasks. While everyone is like this to some extent, it is very marked in children with ADHD.

- **'I don't believe in ADHD – I think it's just an excuse for poor parenting.'** ADHD is not a religion; it is not the prerogative of an individual to believe in it or not. It is a clearly validated, internationally recognised condition that has been acknowledged in the UK by the National Institute for Clinical Excellence (NICE) in its reports in 2000 and 2008. It is a very real and debilitating condition, which is much more common than is generally recognised and can be responsible for long-standing academic, behavioural and social underachievement.

- **'I have seen a child who is subdued or almost a zombie on medication and I don't think children should be on it.'** While a small percentage of children who are treated medically for ADHD can become subdued, it is unusual for this to be the case once there has been careful fine-tuning and adjustment of dosage. In addition, the longer-acting preparations have made this side-effect less likely to occur.

ADHD is a disability

It is helpful for teachers to have a 'disability perspective' and to recognise that ADHD is a neuro-psychological disability of brain function sometimes referred to as a 'hidden handicap'. Children with ADHD have difficulty in achieving the tasks that most people take for granted. It therefore means that accommodations, rather than excuses, need to be made in order to help children achieve to their often very considerable ability. An Individual Education Plan (IEP) for a child with problems can be very helpful. Some children may warrant a Statement of Special Educational Needs. However, this is usually unnecessary unless there are complicating factors. The majority of children with relatively uncomplicated ADHD cope well in a mainstream situation with accommodations.

Historically, concentration difficulties tend to have been viewed under the same umbrella as dyslexia and dyspraxia. Today it is recognised that many conditions of neurodevelopmental dysfunction coexist, which means that many children with specific learning difficulties, such as dyslexia and dyspraxia, may also have difficulties with the core ADHD symptoms of inattentiveness, impulsiveness or hyperactivity. Medical treatment of a child's ADHD, so that he or she is able to concentrate, frequently creates a 'flow-on' improvement in learning or coordination difficulties allowing the therapies for the problems are much more effective.

A child with ADHD may:

- find it difficult to keep up with academic demands;
- need a great deal of support to stay on task and not be distracted;
- be inattentive and thus be poor at following classroom instructions;
- procrastinate and have difficulty following through with tasks and be inconsistent.

All of this can result in a greatly decreased volume of work being done. For other children with ADHD, the verbal impulsiveness may mean that there is frequent calling out in class, and physical impulsiveness may mean other children being hit or punched, or things flicked across the room. High energy levels may also be problematic in the classroom. Frequent complications of difficulties in organisation, planning and time management, and problems with motor planning, coordination and specific learning difficulties may also influence the situation.

Many children with ADHD, who are untreated, become increasingly demoralised; their self-esteem decreases with the struggles they have to face, and they may become depressed or excessively anxious and frustrated. Other children demonstrate aspects of an autistic spectrum disorder, are excessively disruptive, or may have associated emotional and behavioural problems if there are issues within the family, e.g. marital, financial or environmental.

What type of school best suits a child with ADHD?

The general characteristics of a school that is likely to be suitable for a child with ADHD include:

■ an understanding that such children will show a wide range of behaviours and have different learning styles;

■ an informed, whole-school approach to the concept of specific learning difficulties, and especially an understanding of ADHD – an awareness of its existence and its importance, rather than a sceptical approach;

■ the ability to liaise closely between home, school and, where medication is used, medical professionals;

■ an understanding that ADHD is not an excuse, but rather an explanation for troublesome behaviours;

■ where medication is used, an informed understanding of the rationale behind the use of medication, and also that additional strategies will probably be needed;

■ a calm, encouraging and consistent approach, with a well-structured routine and clear rules. Closed-plan rooms, rather than an open and less structured environment, are more appropriate;

■ a good extra-curricular programme;

■ a mechanism for protecting and nurturing a child's self-esteem;

■ screening children who might have emotional, behavioural or educational difficulties at an early age. This should be done as early as possible to prevent progression and before self-esteem, social skills and academic underachievement become problematic;

■ the relevant teacher or SENCO must be in a position to screen and discuss any concerns with parents and, if necessary, to instigate basic educational, academic and behavioural management. This is especially relevant if there is a long wait for a referral or an educational psychology assessment.

The transfer from primary to senior school can be quite problematic for children with ADHD, especially if there are organisational and planning issues. In addition, obtaining feedback from a range of teachers regarding the child's subsequent progress can be more difficult because of the number of teachers involved.

A whole-school approach

Teachers can have a great influence on the general approach to school organisation, curriculum development and personal liaison with parents and other professionals involved with the child. The changes in attitude and understanding must involve the whole school, not just the SENCO. The dinner ladies, school administrative staff and indeed everyone who is involved in the school should have an understanding of the nature of ADHD and its implications.

Teaching style

A teacher who believes in a child, who understands that child's strengths and weaknesses and who nurtures his or her self-esteem is very well placed to positively influence the child's life and is a very valuable asset.

However, the pressure on teachers managing children with severe ADHD can be intense and demanding. Teachers themselves need support and the ability to talk to other informed staff, to be trained in ADHD and related problems and to feel confident that they are handling the child in the most appropriate way.

Teaching strategies for ADHD

Most research of ADHD considers that there is a core deficit in inhibition, which directly impacts on other areas, particularly those involving self-regulation, short-term memory and sequencing. Providing inhibition delay (through medication) tends to allow other executive functions to take place. Other theories consider that inhibition is not of prime importance, but that the problem is primarily of executive function with specific problems with planning, a poor concept of time, and difficulty in organisation, sequencing, working memory and decision making – it has been likened to the way in which the various skills of each individual musician in an orchestra are playing individually without a conductor to coordinate them all.

Among children with ADHD, individual reaction to reinforcement and punishment depends on the level of motivation, the interest level and the different degrees of reinforcement and punishment. Research at the Learning Assessment & Neurocare Centre (LANC) in Sussex, amongst others, confirms what many teachers have known for a long time: the ability to concentrate and to inhibit inappropriate behaviours seems to be context-dependent – many children with ADHD exhibit few such problems when playing computer games. The LANC research shows that inhibitory performance and on-task activity of children with ADHD can be improved when tasks are made more interesting and, in particular, more 'computer game-like'. The addition of narrative, rewards, response costs and coloured characters made a very real difference to children's ability to concentrate and to be better inhibited.

These studies suggest that in order to increase the chances of a child with ADHD maintaining attention and concentration, and of withholding impulsive responses and inappropriate behaviours, the child needs to be adequately motivated and stimulated with a combination of facilitating features and reinforcement strategies. The use of computers appears to be very important and to impact on a child's interests, motivation, stimulation and, thus, level of achievement.

ADHD teaching strategies

- **Teaching should be interactive, innovative, fun and motivating, without over-stimulating the child with ADHD**. Teaching strategies should involve as many senses as possible. Small subtle changes of approach can make the difference between success and failure. Empathy, a sense of humour, patience, believing in the child and the ability to remain unflappable are important.

- **Set boundaries and limits for the child, both in the classroom and playground**. These should be clear, concise and constantly reinforced with limited choices. Have rules written down and regularly point out guidelines and limits. Children then understand exactly where they stand. Make clear what is acceptable and what is not. Have regular daily and weekly routines and forewarn the child of any changes. The use of contracts, lists and reminders may also be helpful.

'Being fair' does not necessarily require that all children are treated identically. Rules and expectations may need to be individualised, but should be applied fairly and consistently. This does not mean that children with ADHD should not be accountable for their actions; they should have to comply with the rules, which have been tailored to their needs, and be able to achieve what is expected of them. The threat of punishment actually has very little influence in deterring the child from breaking the rule, since their understanding of cause and effect is poor.

- **Classroom setting is important**. Open-plan classrooms pose considerable problems for children with ADHD, allowing them to be easily distracted. The child with ADHD needs to be seated near the front of the room, in a position where the distractions can be minimised, close to the teacher and, if possible, another pupil who would be a good role model. Increasing the distance between desks may also minimise distraction. Children with ADHD perform better in a small class or a one-to-one situation.

- **Instructions should be repeated if necessary and given clearly and frequently**. Face the children, make eye contact first and keep instructions as concise, brief and clear as possible. Give one instruction at a time to avoid overwhelming the child. Instructions may need to be repeated and rules written down. State consequences clearly and fairly.

Develop a private signal or cue for the child to start on a task, or other strategies. Positive instructions, such as 'put your feet on the floor' rather than 'don't put your feet on the desk' will have more effect. Make it clear that it is the behaviour that is not acceptable, not the child. Don't give instructions until the class is quiet and everyone is listening. Many children with ADHD have problems with auditory instructions and, if dyslexic, may also have problems with visual instructions. Therefore, write the key points down as well as discussing them. Check that the instructions or topic have been understood.

Addressing coexisting features

As most children with ADHD have a number of coexisting or complicating features, it is important to address these once the core ADHD symptoms have been taken into account. Key among these coexisting problems are:

1   **Specific learning difficulties**
    Support may involve using specific dyslexia-type programmes, one-to-one support to help with phonics, the use of computerized learning techniques, etc.

2   **Support for planning, organisation and time management**
    These are executive function difficulties and frequently persist despite adequate treatment of the core ADHD symptoms. Many children with ADHD have a very poor concept of time and thus are often late and appear disorganised. These children benefit from help in time management, planning and organisation, and having an ADHD coach can be very helpful here. Colour coordinated folders, having a school–home diary, strategies for remembering homework, planning the days and week ahead, etc. are essential here.

3   **Disruptive Behavioural Disorder**
    This includes those children with Oppositional Defiant Disorder and Oppositional Defiant Disorder and Conduct Disorder. Children with this condition have persistent behavioural difficulties despite being managed effectively for their ADHD. They need very strict behavioural and educational strategies, and at times may be helped by the use of additional medications to try to mellow their disruptive behavioural disorder difficulties.

4   **Ongoing emotional and behavioural difficulties**
    If these result from family issues, specific counselling/psychological therapies may be helpful. For example, in a child who has ADHD and attachment difficulties emanating from issues relating to adoption and/or earlier abuse, counselling can be very helpful.

5   **Persistently low self-esteem or demoralisation**
    This usually improves when the ADHD is treated. However, if it does not, extra supports may be necessary. Some children with these issues are more likely to be involved in bullying or self-harm.

6   **Autistic spectrum features**
    These may include poor social communication, over-focused interests, lack of empathy or poor eye contact. There is a range of autistic spectrum difficulties, the commonest of which in this context is Asperger's Syndrome. Autistic spectrum difficulties can coexist with ADHD, and the extent of their impact on a child is often hard to assess until the child's ADHD symptoms and other medically treatable conditions have been managed effectively.

7   **Developmental Coordination Disorder (DCD)/dyspraxia/ disorders of attention and motor perception (DAMP)**
    Up to 50% of children with ADHD also have a DCD. Poor motor coordination affects many aspects of school life – slowness of dressing, changing for sports, sports themselves and interaction on the playground. It is also seen in the classroom as the 'clumsy child' who bumps into things, knocks over his or her chair and fails to clap in rhythm to the school song. The most common problem seen in the classroom is with handwriting. Research shows that

children with both ADHD and DCD have a psychosocially poorer outcome than those with ADHD alone. They need special attention, which usually involves treating the ADHD appropriately and then providing appropriate remedial attention for learning and coordination difficulties.

For example, if a child is still having considerable problems with handwriting, a paediatric occupational therapy assessment should be sought to ascertain which of the skill areas mentioned above are deficient. Suitable strategies can then be planned to support classroom learning. These may involve strategies to improve the child's sensory integration. This is a specialised therapy that builds on the child's sensory experience, which in turn can improve both motor and academic performance. Other children will need help with their visual perceptual skills (how the brain interprets what the eye sees), their visual motor skills (how the hand and eyes work together) or their fine motor skills (how their hands work). Some work is done directly with the child, and some by the suggestion of strategies for use at home or at school.

Problems with handwriting

A child who is asked to manipulate a pencil before he or she has the necessary control of the movements of the finger joints may, typically, hold forcefully onto the pencil for stability (frequently breaking the lead) and write using the movements of the whole hand. This fisted grip means of holding the pencil initially helps to overcome the child's problems, but this may become a habit and the child may continue to use it even when they have the maturation and ability to use their finger joints. The result is often immature writing and a painful hand.

Handwriting is a complicated learning task: the child has to have mastered certain levels of visual-perceptual, visual-motor, gross and fine motor skills. They must have adequate sensori-motor foundations, motor planning and spatial awareness. On top of this they must have the cognitive and language ability to organise ideas, express them appropriately and understand the rules of grammar and syntax. All of this assumes that they have been able to pay attention and learn the skill as taught by the teacher.

The three Ps of handwriting

POSTURE

Make sure that the child has a chair and table/desk that is appropriate. His or her feet should be on the floor; ankles, knees, hips and elbows should be as close to right angles as possible. Good posture provides the stability to the child's body that can then allow the mobility of the hand. A slightly sloped writing surface encourages extension at the wrists and improves dexterity. This can be accomplished by attaching the child's exercise book to a closed two- or three-inch ring binder with the raised edge away from the child. A piece of non-slip rubber mat on the bottom prevents the file from moving about on the desk.

PAPER

This needs to be positioned correctly so that the child can see what he or she is writing. Imagine the child sitting with both elbows on the desk with hands together so that they form a right angle – the right-handed child should align the top of the paper with the left arm in this position and the left-handed child should align it with the right arm. A piece of masking tape on the desk to remind child and teacher of the paper position can be useful. This is extremely important for left-handed students who frequently develop a 'hooked hand' when writing on poorly positioned paper, in order to see what they are writing. The paper needs to be of good enough quality that writing is a pleasing experience, whatever implement is used.

PENCIL / PEN

This needs to be a good quality tool that works for the child. A pencil with a larger shaft is easier to manipulate. The younger child will need repeated prompting to hold the pencil with the 'proper grip'. The important aspect of the grip is that there is a space between the thumb and the first finger so that the pencil can be moved by the thumb and first finger in opposition to each other, with the second finger providing support under the pencil. If the space between the thumb and first finger is closed, as in a child fisting the hand around the pencil, then increasing the size of the pencil shaft should help. The shaft can be increased by using a pencil grip or by taping three pencils together with the writing one slightly longer than the other two. A felt-tip handwriting pen may be easier for a child with a heavy grip who frequently breaks pencil leads. The best quality coloured pencils, markers or crayons should be used to minimise the frustration experience for the child.

Correcting pencil grips: once the child has habituated a less-than-functional grip (usually by the age of seven), it is very hard to change. However, many go on to write successfully with very strange grips that may well cause problems in later life, but which are adequate in these days of computers.

Computers are often the long-term answer to illegible handwriting, but learning keyboard skills can be just as frustrating for a child because they require good fine motor and motor planning skills. Until a student can type at a minimum of 20 words per minute, using a computer is no less frustrating than using a pencil. A good typing program for the computer used regularly, little and often (e.g. 15 minutes, five times a week) is the most effective method of learning. A reward system built in by the parents to give immediate rewards for successful participation with the program will be the most effective method. Generally, a laptop computer for a student with ADHD in the class-room is an expensive risk and an added distraction. Cheaper solutions are available such as the portable word processor, the AlphaSmart (www.AlphaSmart.com) or similar.

Another classroom recommendation is to modify the amount that the ADHD and DCD student needs to write. Try to use creative solutions including involving other students as note-takers, allowing the student to dictate answers, using speech-enabled computer software. Teachers have to balance the need to know what the child knows with insisting on the written word being the only way to express this knowledge. Typically, the child who has problems with handwriting is very aware of his lack of skill and will try to avoid it. The risk is that they have a paragraph of knowledge in their heads but are only prepared to put a sentence on paper. Like all aspects of learning, a sense of success builds self-confidence and encourages new learning. The challenge for the teacher is to find a way for poor writers to feel successful, while encouraging them to improve.

Troubleshooting in the classroom

For some children additional strategies are necessary over and above the more basic management strategies for a child with ADHD. Below are some common classroom scenarios, with suggestions for strategies that may be helpful for teachers.

The diagnosis of ADHD has been made in a child, but there are persistent difficulties with impulsive behavioural comments or actions and poor concentration.

If medication is not being used, it is possible that it should be. If it is, then dosage or timing adjustments should be made. Teacher feedback to the child's parents and doctor/specialist is essential in order to develop the optimum dosage regime.

The core ADHD symptoms are well contained, but there are persistent problems with planning, organisation and time management.

The best strategy is to try to minimise the impact of a child's disorganisation on his or her schooling and life difficulties. Specific strategies – such as working with the home, having home–school diaries, foreshadowing situations, colour-coding books, etc. – are necessary here. A coach or mentor can also be very helpful.

The child's core ADHD symptoms are satisfactorily controlled, but he still finds it hard to write things down.

Consider whether there may be associated developmental coordination difficulties or problems with coordination and visual processing. An occupational therapist might help. Sometimes the problem in writing things down is due to boredom . . . ('Why should I bother writing it down if I can say it straight away?') and sometimes due to short-term memory issues. Frequently, improving typing skills and then working on the computer is helpful in this situation.

Concentration improves but there are still problems with short-term memory.

Usually, additional changes in medication will not make a great deal of difference and it is important that tight educational strategies be implemented, utilising the best means of processing information for the child, i.e. visual or auditory.

The child can concentrate on Lego, computers and other things of interest, but will not, or cannot, concentrate on the subjects which are less interesting.

Anyone can concentrate better on things that are interesting, but ADHD children seem to have a faulty 'on–off switch' and are unable to switch on for the less interesting subjects. Generally, adjustments to medication can be helpful in this situation. It is important not to extrapolate and assume that because a child is able to concentrate on interesting subjects, he or she should then be able to concentrate on anything.

The child's core ADHD symptoms are well contained, but there is persistent oppositionality, arguing, defying and pushing the boundaries of school discipline.

Consider whether the child may have associated Oppositional Defiant Disorder. This is usually, but not always, more of a problem in the home rather than in the school, but it would be worth asking parents about this. In many cases, when the core ADHD symptoms are treated, the Oppositional Defiant Disorder symptoms and Conduct Disorder symptoms also improve. However, there are many children where this does not happen, and if reasonable behavioural strategies have not been effective there is an increasing tendency to use a second, additional medication to try to mellow the oppositionality. Generally, self-esteem and social skills will not improve until this is done.

Despite adequate treatment, self-esteem remains low and motivation poor, and the child continues to be demoralised.

Consider whether the core ADHD symptoms are, in fact, adequately treated. If so, then consider whether the child might be depressed or have other complications or environmental difficulties that are not being fully addressed. Sometimes it becomes more apparent with time that there is evidence of associated autistic spectrum difficulties coexisting with the child's ADHD, i.e. difficulty in socialising appropriately, lack of eye contact, lack of empathy and/or ritualistic or obsessive behaviours. Also consider whether the child's environment could be more supportive and nurturing and whether the child's 'islets of competence' are being satisfactorily sought and rewarded.

The classroom situation is satisfactory but there are problems at playtime and at lunchtime.

Consider whether medication may be wearing off in the unstructured times. Consider also whether, prior to diagnosis and treatment, a child's name may have gone before him or her due to a time when they were more impulsive or oppositional. If it is considered that the child's ADHD is managed effectively, consider using a play buddy, investigate the possibility of bullying and try to find playground activities that might hold the child's interest.

The child's ADHD appears to be adequately treated but he or she continues to learn at a relatively slow rate.

Consider whether an Educational Psychology evaluation would be helpful. It is useful to know what expectations are reasonable for a child: is he or she of high or low IQ? Are there any coexisting specific learning difficulties? In most cases this will already have been appraised at the initial assessment, but the profile of the child can change once ADHD is managed effectively. Children with ADHD and specific learning difficulties need support for both problems, and the child may well need specific support for his or her dyslexia or other learning difficulty.

The child appears to be sad, miserable and possibly depressed, despite the ADHD being treated.

Discuss the situation with the parents and consider whether there are any other issues at school such as bullying or unidentified learning difficulties that may be impacting on the situation. If the sadness continues then the child's medical practitioner might wish to consider whether an antidepressant should be prescribed. Occasionally, manic depression (bipolar disorder) can coexist with ADHD. In the more inattentive-only form of ADHD, which occurs especially in girls, depression is a frequent coexisting condition.

It is considered that the child might have ADHD, but the parents are not at all interested in this possibility.

Try to explain to the parents exactly what issues you are seeing in the classroom; encourage them to become better informed on ADHD and related conditions and to ignore the myth and misinformation which have been so prevalent in the lay press. Explain that you consider that the child has potential but is underachieving and/or has behavioural or other symptoms whihc might be consistent with ADHD. It is important that concerns about treatment do not obscure the route to diagnosis.

The child is gifted but underachieving relative to ability.

Consider whether the child is bored and is not being challenged sufficiently. Consider whether the fact that the child can concentrate on the interesting subjects, but not on the boring ones, might mean that he or she is being under-treated medically. Help from the National Association for Able Students might be useful, as might a recognition of the child's true ability, and measures put in place to try to achieve these.

As a teacher, you feel you are doing all you can for a child and yet things are still not working out.

Develop a dialogue with the medical practitioner treating the child so that, together with the parents, you can make decisions about why things are not working out. Problems may arise from:

- insufficient doses of medication;
- the lack of use of an additional medication to treat complications such as depression or Oppositional Defiant Disorder;
- a lack of understanding of the basic nature of ADHD and thus a less than adequate implementation of teaching strategies;
- the fact that the child has persistent planning, organisation and time management difficulties which will probably not respond to additional medications.

7 Other tips that teachers might find helpful

Not all children with ADHD respond to straightforward strategies as previously mentioned. This chapter contains some suggestions for more complex cases. For example, if a child is receiving recurrent detentions, try and look at what is causing these and whether appropriate accommodations might prevent them. For example if it is an issue to do with homework then very frequently this is because the child's medication has worn off, because he or she has not written the homework down, or because he or she is disorganised and cannot get the homework back to school. Appropriate accommodations can minimise the occurrence of this. Most children with ADHD do not learn from detentions. Some even use detentions as a means of avoiding specific task or demands.

- Try to ignore minimal negative behaviours and try distracting the child onto something else as a means of re-engaging his or her focus. For example, he or she could be asked to move to a different place in the class, the activity could be broken up with some exercise, or allowed a brief time out. Non-verbal feedback, cards or prompts can also be helpful.

- Unstructured times, particularly breaktimes and lunchtimes can cause difficulties in part because the child with ADHD has to organise his or her behaviour and negotiate subtle social interactions. Preparing a child for these changes, giving him or her a particular role or rewarding activity, or using the time as an alternative for doing homework can sometimes help. Using a lunch buddy could be trialled. Using behaviour report cards that link what happens at school with the home is also very useful. This can be helpful both for the playground situation and for the academic side of things.

- What may appear to be attention-seeking behaviour is often impulsiveness in children with ADHD. These children are often 'in your face', they cannot wait, they want things now, they interrupt your conversations, blurt out the answers, and often appear to go on and on and on until they get your attention. These types of difficulties can be quite exhausting. Try and reward appropriate behaviour only with your attention, try and minimise the time between the achievement or problem occurring and the praise or punishment that ensues. The longer the delay, the more likely the child with ADHD will forget or not see the relevance of the praise or punishment to the original situation.

- Children with ADHD find it particularly difficult to plan ahead, and also to cope with new or changed situations. Having a class timetable that is written down, and as much as possible trying to foreshadow any changes that might occur is important. Many children with ADHD will need time to adjust and to assimilate new information about a change from what has been until now a routine. If they are also anxious it is sometimes best not to tell them till the change is just about to happen. Speaking to parents can often give guidance on how best such situations might be handled.

- Whilst everyone has good and bad days, children with ADHD tend to have very good days and very bad days. There is usually no obvious reason for this, not usually related to things that have been going on in their lives, their diet or any other reason, and this makes teaching these children and finding a level on which to standardise things quite difficult. The inconsistency is an inherent part of many children's ADHD and it is helpful to recognise and to take this into consideration in developing teaching strategies.

- Many children with ADHD are less flexible and adaptable and tend to get more readily frustrated than their peers. This means that they are more likely to have prolonged tantrums and sudden outbursts, and to be physically or verbally aggressive, often in response to apparently minor difficulties. Such problems frequently impact on the child's interaction with parents, teachers, siblings and peers. If such problems are persistent, it is a good idea to analyse the context in which they occur and the time of day, and to then look at trying to put in place appropriate strategies and accommodations. If they still persist then it may be worthwhile looking at more effective management of the child's ADHD overall.

- Quite frequently subtle changes of approach and strategy or a voice tone can reduce the stress of a situation and promote a more positive relationship with the child with ADHD. It is often quite surprising how often the combination of warmth, patience and humour, together with consistency and firmness, will go a long way to counteracting the rejection and criticism that these children so often experience.

- Nurturing and supportive self-esteem is critical to effective management of ADHD. Sometimes there have been many years of criticism, punishment and blame and the child has been repeatedly told he or she is a failure, eventually coming to believe this. Handling the child and particularly very carefully punishing the child where appropriate is essential to avoid exacerbation of problematic self-esteem. Rephrasing commands or communications in a positive way can make all the difference. Encouraging positive self-esteem is vital in children with ADHD. Many children with the condition have become increasingly demoralised and demotivated and the struggle they have had with the schoolwork and social interaction over the years has usually meant that their self-esteem, motivation and usually social skills have become quite problematic. Careful listening, sharing and caring can help make the child feel valued and have a sense of loyalty and responsibility to the larger group encouraged. Try and get the child to contribute and feel connected to the group, and find something they are good at. Encourage their 'islets of competence', and find something relevant even though it may appear rather trivial, that the child is good at and can do on a regular basis to contribute. Remember to praise him or her for commitment and efforts to become a valued member of the group. Try and recognise the child's innate potential, and use this as a way of nurturing self-esteem, putting less emphasis on the things that go wrong. Try and play to the child's strengths and use this to enable him or her to accomplish smaller tasks. Try and encourage independence and adopt an empathetic supportive approach to his or her views. Support him or her in activities that are both within and outside the school and praise and acknowledge even apparently minor achievements.

- If the child's rate of learning remains persistently low despite his or her ADHD being effectively managed, consider whether the child may have other associated difficulties. For example, about a third of children with ADHD have coexisting specific learning difficulties or problems with developmental coordination disorder. Such children need support in all areas. The child's physician may need to review the situation with regard to whether or not the child's medical management is appropriate and has been carefully fine-tuned; they may also wish to consider whether hearing or vision might need rechecking, and/or whether or not there may be some other medical condition that is impacting on the problems. It is always important to consider whether or not the child's core ADHD symptoms are satisfactorily controlled and to ascertain that the child is concentrating well and is not being excessively hyperactive or impulsive. Containing these symptoms is essential to effective management. Frequently a minor change of attitude or of supportive strategy can make all the difference to a child.

- The appropriate use of behaviour management techniques very much depends on the age of the child and whether there is associated inherent oppositionality. Agreeing on basic classroom rules so that you can fall back on these rather than taking each argument in its own right can be very important. Ignoring minor behavioural infringements but only concentrating on the more serious ones is essential as is praising the positive behaviours and choosing one's battles wisely. Giving commands carefully without too many, obtaining eye contact to make them take notice, and stating the consequences clearly is important. Token reward systems can be helpful, contracts are sometimes helpful, and foreshadowing a specific problem/situation and trying to either avoid or anticipate what is likely to happen can also be very useful.

- Reprimands and punishments should be done with care and sensitivity as many children with ADHD are hypersensitive and tend to misinterpret comments. Use careful reprimands with a measured tone of voice and attitude suited to the behaviour. Make it clear that it is not the child you are criticising, rather the behaviour. Don't see the child as a failure but look forward to doing things more positively next time and suggest how the situation might happen differently in the future.

- In those oppositional children, particularly those who are not keen to communicate, who had frequent outbursts of temper and rages, public outbursts are counter-productive to both you and the pupil. Therefore try and give him or her the option of not losing face, develop non-verbal strategies and focus on what has gone wrong, rather than the pupil him or herself. You may have to say the same message in a calm non-confrontational tone, over and over again, using the 'broken record technique' and if possible use distracting strategies; try and avoid using the somewhat accusatory term 'you', particularly as such children are usually very sensitive to criticism or comment and easily misinterpret or overreact.

- Bullying is a common problem for children with ADHD. They often bully others, partly because of their aggression and also their impulsiveness, as well as the fact that they want to be able to be seen as part of the group, because of their social skills difficulties. However, they may also be easily led and sometimes set up by other children to do the bullying. The others often run for cover and the ADHD child can take the whole blame. A child who has been bullied may often have low self-esteem and other associated difficulties.

- Pupils with ADHD are much more likely to be suspended or excluded from school. Compulsory assessment for conditions such as ADHD should be done in any such situation, as is currently the case in the United States. The simplistic assumption that disruptive behaviour leading to exclusion, is solely the result of family dysfunction or socioeconomic difficulties and is usually not appropriate. Persistent problems with planning, organisation and time management, irrespective of whether or not a child is taking medication, are frequent problems in the school setting. Difficulties with prioritising, making decisions, thinking and planning ahead, and having a concept of time passing are common difficulties. They may cause a great deal of difficulty in a school setting, and most children with such executive function-type difficulties benefit from accommodations. They are the sort of difficulties that many teachers consider are very much within a child's own volition; however, unfortunately in this group of children that appears not to be the case. Having a poor concept of time, with the associated difficulties in planning to the future, setting priorities and carrying through a long-term project to completion are particularly challenging for pupils with ADHD. This particularly applies to getting homework to and from school, getting it written down and organised, and strategies such as a home–school diary, e-mailing the homework back to the teacher, and enlisting support of parents can all be helpful.

- Homework is a particular difficultly for children with ADHD. As mentioned, problems in planning, organisation and time management, together with other difficulties such as problems with writing, learning or memory, can all make this increasingly problematic. In addition, if medication is being used, it usually wears off towards the end of the school day. It is generally helpful to try and avoid giving homework at the end of the class when the pupil with ADHD has lost focus and is preparing to move on. Having a regular daily routine to get the homework back to school and having ongoing liaison with parents is important. Short-term memory problems, over and above concentration difficulties, can be a particular problem in children with ADHD. Very frequently the short-term memory problems persist even if the concentration is effectively managed. These children tend to benefit from having a general outline of the new information given to them initially to guide their attention and progress, to have instructions or new information repeated or given from a different angle, from having established eye contact with the pupil prior to giving instructions and to ensure that he or she is listening carefully, as well as breaking down a task or information into small steps or chunks, and considering altering the rate of presentation of new material where appropriate.

- The weak focus of a child with ADHD means that benefit is usually seen by frequently changing tasks on which he has to concentrate, by having frequent short breaks, by asking the child a question or getting him to do something every now and again to make sure he is focusing and to avoid lengthy tasks, particularly those he is seen as tedious or monotonous. If these have to be done, disperse them with either frequent breaks or more engaging tasks. When children with ADHD have associated specific learning difficulties they may need additional educational support via being on the special needs support register. For example, they may need additional reading time if their reading is weak. The term 'dyslexia' is used less these days, but it relates to a language-based learning difficulty specifically related to reading. It is probably helpful to think of specific weaknesses in reading, maths, spelling, writing, etc. rather than using the label of dyslexia too globally. Children with dyslexia are helped by being taught phonological awareness, sound discrimination/identification, syllables and rhyme, and hearing sounds within words. They benefit from a range of different accommodations to suit their learning style. For example, visual learners benefit by using plenty of visual materials, overhead projectors, video and interactive whiteboards. Auditory learners find discussions, questions and answers, word pictures and auditory memory games helpful. Kinaesthetic learners like to gather information in lots of different ways, and to further do things in a hands-on and experimental way. Students who struggle with written work may eventually benefit from doing touch-typing using a computer, using a tape recorder or dictaphone or scribe or possibly using voice recognition software.

- Frequently a child's name has gone before him or her because of the things that have gone wrong prior to the effective management of his or her ADHD. This means that he or she may be blamed for things inappropriately, and scapegoated by teachers who assume he or she has done something wrong, even though this may not be the case. Frequently child–teacher relationships have completely broken down. A child needs to know that someone is on their side who believes in them and who is not a soft touch, but rather will support the child, will say no when no is meant, and who will discipline consistently and nurture their self-esteem within defined boundaries. Try and avoid taking away things as punishment that the child does well. A child with ADHD would generally not see the connection in any case but taking away the things in which the child excels is likely to further exacerbate the child's problematic self-esteem. There is a fine line between providing appropriate accommodations for the child and promoting self-reliance, as compared to doing things excessively for the child.

- Persistent social skills difficulties may be caused by impulsiveness, by dogmatism or rigid thinking and by poor listening skills or lack of focus. Sometimes having associated features of Asperger's Syndrome exacerbates the situation and also their high energy levels may make it difficult for their peers to keep up with them. In children with uncomplicated ADHD, in most occasions when the ADHD is effectively medically managed, social skills improve. If not, reconsideration of whether or not the child might have Asperger's Syndrome coexisting with the ADHD may be worthwhile. Other strategies such as using social skills groups and one-to-one social skills support with review of things that have gone right and may have gone wrong can be helpful. Using a study buddy for activities and projects may be helpful, and enlisting the support of peers in the classroom, especially those with good social awareness, may also be helpful.

- Always aim to play to the child's strengths as much as possible. Identify the positive attributes of the pupils with ADHD. Possibly use the analogy of a mountain range where there are peaks and valleys: the peaks representing their skills and the valleys representing the areas of ADHD in which they have difficulty. Aim to try and strengthen the peaks and minimise the depths of the valleys with effective management. The tendency to think unconventionally and to have obvious enthusiasm together with high energy levels in many pupils with ADHD can make them extremely interesting and intriguing in the school setting. Channelling and encouraging these attributes correctly can make all the difference to the way in which a child with ADHD develops and how effective he or she may become in society. Aim to focus on the positives rather than the negatives and consider how the negatives may be viewed as strengths. A distractible child, for example, may be perceived as one who is curious and questioning. Impulsiveness may make children more energetic or decisive. Many such children thrive on tasks that require high energy levels, dogmatic behaviour, being busy and having lots of stamina. Such children may respond well to having responsibility in groups or with specific tasks.

- Monitoring progress is always essential and should be done in conjunction with the child's physician if the child is on medication. There are a number of school feedback forms available, all of which are aimed at having some gauge of change in the child's concentration, distractibility, procrastination and organisation as well as impulsiveness and overactivity. Most charts also monitor self-esteem, conversation skills, anxiety and academic progress. Good liaison and communication between all professionals caring for the child is essential.

- The child who has ADHD but who also is in the gifted and talented category may appear to be of average or lower abilities without his or her true strengths and weaknesses being fully recognised. In the wrong type of schooling environment, a gifted child can sometimes present with symptoms suggestive of ADHD, and such consideration is always important for the physician in the differential diagnosis. Such children may have a significant scatter of abilities and there is some evidence that educational psychology tests, in a child with ADHD, can underestimate a child's true ability because of the concentrational and short-term memory weaknesses. Such children often have a 'spiky profile' with very significant cognitive strengths but often having real problems with social skills, concentration, organisation, short-term memory or self-esteem. Gifted children with ADHD tend to often become demoralised and have lower self-esteem at an earlier age than the more average child with ADHD. Their chronic boredom can be a real challenge to teachers as average things just do not interest them. It could often be a mistake to place a gifted and talented child with ADHD in a lower set as this takes away the challenge and exacerbates the boredom and thus the demotivation and low self-esteem. Such children are often said to have dual disabilities: on the one hand they may need to be on the gifted and talented register and on the other on a special needs register.

- Some parents refuse to accept or they deny that their child may have a problem even if that is very obvious to the teacher. This places the teacher in an invidious situation particularly as some parents may blame the teacher for their child's problem. In such situations it is usually helpful for the teacher to try and explain carefully to the parents exactly what difficulties are being seen in the classroom, encourage them to become better informed about conditions such as ADHD and to try and dispel the myths and misinformation that have been so prevalent around these subjects. Sometimes the difficulties occur because the parents have had similar problems at school themselves, as conditions like ADHD are highly genetic. This means that such problems have become the norm for them. If parents still refuse to accept that the child may have difficulties, keeping a joint diary at home and school over the next month or two is sometimes helpful to assist with reassessment of the situation subsequently. It may be helpful to encourage the parents to visit the child's general practitioner, or involve the special needs teacher and/or school doctor.

■ The extensive myth and misinformation surrounding the condition and the medications used to treat it have influenced not only parents but also many teachers. Some teachers therefore find that their colleagues may be sceptical and particularly in the senior school there may be some teachers who accept ADHD is a valid condition and some who are still inappropriately sceptical. This places the informed teachers in a difficult situation and may mean that the child receives different supports in different subjects. Given that the various reports including the NICE report (www.nice.org.uk) have validated that ADHD is an internationally recognised complex neurobiological disorder, it is increasingly inappropriate for teachers to have sceptical views of this common condition. Indeed ADHD affects up to 5% of the UK school population. Researchers believe that people with ADHD have a few structures within their brain that are smaller and that their neurotransmitters/the chemical messages in the brain/do not work properly. In dealing with teachers in this situation, it may be helpful to encourage colleagues to attend in-service training and to collect some informed reading material for them.

■ The children with ADHD that coexists with the early onset of Oppositional Defiant Disorder act as 'teenagers before their time'. Such behaviour can be extremely worrying for teachers as well as for parents. It may be malicious but is often impulsive. Mornings can be particularly difficult and if it persists despite the child being on medication then it is worthwhile discussing this with the child's physician. Don't assume that the problems in behaviour are automatically due to inadequate parenting; a child with severe ADHD, particularly with associated Oppositional Defiant Disorder, causes very significant family dysfunction. Parents and also siblings may become extremely stressed. This can sometimes correct the erroneous impression of family difficulties being the cause of the child's behaviour and the assumption that the problems must be due to inadequate parenting. However, it is usually the reverse in that the child's innate difficult behaviour causes very significant family dysfunction. Be aware of the reality of suffering, living with ADHD, and remember that a child with ADHD will stand out as being different from his or her siblings and peers at all stages of his or her development. Such parents often dread going to the school in case there has been another disaster and to be further blamed for their child's difficulties. The transition from primary to secondary school is often a tipping point for things to go wrong in a child with ADHD. Frequently, particularly if the child is bright, he or she may have coped well at primary school, particularly where there was only one teacher and few changes and with fewer organisational demands.

■ With the transition to senior school, the work becomes harder, there are many more demands on the child with ADHD and their inherent weaknesses with organisational and time management. Changing friendships and social issues may also become problematic. Using a coach or mentor, having a good form tutor, being able to sit down with the child and use a timetable and plan ahead, and good liaison between primary and secondary school are all important.

■ In a similar way the transition to Sixth Form College after GCSEs is also a difficult time. This can be particularly problematic if the child is going from a structured school environment, to a much less structured Sixth Form College environment. At this stage it is particularly the lack of structure, together with sometimes mixing with the wrong company, being unsure as to long-term motivation, being involved in drink or drugs and being easily led by peers that can all contribute to the difficulties. Good communication between school and college, insisting on a college which is as structured as possible, and using good role models are all helpful.

■ Transition on to university is another difficult time. The even more significant lack of structure at many universities is a particular problem. However, in part to counteract this, universities generally tend to have good special needs provision and frequently coaches or mentors, laptops and other dictating equipment are available. As much as possible it is usually beneficial for youth with ADHD to go into a course which they like and which is as structured as possible, continuing recognition of the fact that in very many cases ADHD is a lifespan condition and that the problems are not outgrown just because the child leaves school. In particular, gifted youth with ADHD who are progressing to university frequently have major problems with organisation and this needs to be addressed with as much structure and 'scaffolding' as possible.

■ Occasionally children use their ADHD as an excuse and/or parents have worked hard to gain support for their child and that support appears to be excessive. It is always important that ADHD is seen as an explanation and not an excuse. The best way of doing this is to involve the child in his or her overall management and to treat him or her in a mature way, explaining the condition and the strategies used to treat it as appropriately as possible. If a child seems to be using his or her ADHD as an excuse or as a way of opting out of things, this needs to be discussed with him or her and is often related to their loss of confidence, or the child's academic underachievement relative to ability being not fully recognised. Spending time discussing the reasons why the child is felt to have ADHD, and looking at strategies and ways forward are usually very beneficial in this setting.

■ Remember to differentiate between ADHD and ADD. Although ADHD is the broad term to cover all categories of inattentiveness, hyperactivity and impulsiveness, in practice, in educational circles it is best to use the term ADHD for those children who are hyperactive, impulsive and inattentive, and to use ADD for those children who are daydreamers, 'away with the fairies', and who are inattentive rather than behaviourally difficult. Particularly if they are bright and are girls, the inattentiveness is sometimes not recognised and such children tend to fade away in class. They also often have problems with anxiety, depression, mood swings and low self-esteem.

■ Useful websites include www.myadhd.com, www.helpforadhd.org, www.chadd.org, www.addiss.co.uk, www.adders.org and www.gifteddevelopment.com.

■ The overall school ethos is critical to the management of a child with ADHD and often only slight changes of approach can make a huge difference to the child. Also the teacher's attitude in front of his peers is important.

■ Remember that many children with ADHD present in different ways and some may be more behaviourally difficult, some may be more moody, some may have more of a learning problem or more social problems. This really depends on the extent of which the core features, of hyperactivity, impulsiveness or inattentiveness present in an individual child and to what extent the complications have occurred. Children with ADHD benefit from not being ridiculed, from positive things being found about them, from having a positive role such as even being the 'goldfish monitor' or similar and from having good role models. The child's confidentiality should always be respected and if the child is on medication during the day, confidential and discrete arrangements should be made.

- Pupils with ADHD benefit from using well-designed worksheets, from not being overwhelmed by having too much information on any one page, and often by using computers as much as possible.

The long-term outlook

ADHD creates a significant vulnerability and makes the person more likely to experience problems later in life. Such issues include academic underachievement, social, 'relationship problems and difficulties in family functioning, low self-esteem, employment, and mood and anxiety disorders. For some, especially those who have disruptive and antisocial difficulties early in life, there is an increased incidence of entry to the criminal justice system and substance abuse.

However, the wide range of presentations of people with ADHD, the variability in coexisting conditions and the differing environments have made it hard to judge the outcome for any one particular person with ADHD. There are a number of studies now – mostly on the shorter term – which, combined with wide clinical experience, indicate that many features of ADHD can be helped effectively; and the long-term outlook for the majority of people who are treated in a finely managed way can be a great deal better than if that person is not treated at all. This very much agreed with the improvements usually seen in the majority of people treated in clinical practice.

The initial management aim for anyone of school age with ADHD is to enable them to get through their school years as intact as possible. This means that, at the very minimum, the child's self-esteem, academic and social skills must be protected so that he or she finishes school doing as well as possible in these areas. Frequently, once someone with ADHD has found a career pathway that interests them, what in the past has been a problem or a handicap can become a very positive characteristic.

Some children with ADHD appear to outgrow it by the end of their school years, especially if they are diagnosed and treated early. The majority benefit from medication during their school years; as adults they may be unable to concentrate on boring subjects or might still be impulsive, but usually their lives are much better, either on or off medication, than if they had not been treated. Today, adult ADHD is widely recognised as being a valid condition, and there is clear evidence that at least 70% of cases have significant ADHD symptoms persisting into adulthood.

As with the medical treatment of any condition, the long-term use of any medication needs to be monitored constantly and any concerns about side-effects must be balanced against benefits obtained. ADHD is not a static condition and, unfortunately, progresses, untreated, with time. Children should always be under regular specialist review, and regular decisions should be made on whether or not the benefits of medication warrant continuation of treatment.

In the UK, a study from the Bedford Group for Life Course and Statistical Studies looked at adult outcomes of ADHD, using the 1970 British cohort following all children born in Great Britain in the first week of April 1970. It showed that those who had ADHD at age 10 were significantly more likely than those without ADHD to face a wide range of negative outcomes in adulthood, especially in the areas of

> Treating ADHD in children aims to protect their self-esteem, academic and social skills, enabling them to achieve to their potential at school.

> Clinical experience shows that with careful long-term management, almost all children with ADHD of a wide range of presentations and severity can be helped.

> Carefully controlled studies on the treatment of ADHD show clear improvement in behaviour and learning with a decrease in overactivity.

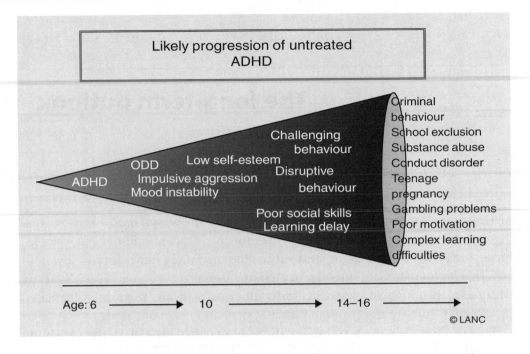

Figure 8.1 Likely progression of untreated ADHD

The Bedford Group study found that men and women who had ADHD at age 10 were more likely to be:

- unqualified or with low levels of qualifications;

- living in a low socioeconomic situation;

- living in a workless household;

- living in temporary accommodation;

- single, separated or divorced;

- cigarette smokers;

- dissatisfied with their lives;

- depressed or have drug problems.

social exclusion, education, economic status, housing, relationships, crime and health. It showed that men tended to fare less well and were specifically at greater risk of homelessness, more serious offending, being the victims of assault, having alcohol-related problems, obsessive life behaviour and having psychiatric disturbance by age 30. Women, on the other hand, were at greater risk of earning a low income, being a single parent and living in a workless household. Also, 2% of the sample had not experienced any of the 24 negative outcomes, thus suggesting that there is a group of people with ADHD who have a resilience to the problems it creates. This is borne out by clinical experience.

So far, no studies have investigated the long-term effects. However, clinical experience shows that in a good environment, especially where the child has a reasonable IQ, such children usually respond to a modest dose of medication, and most progress into adulthood fairly well, provided there are no associated severe learning, anxiety or depressive difficulties.

On the other hand, children with the more hyperactive symptoms – especially if there is the associated early onset of disruptive behaviour disorder – are at more risk, even with treatment, of having an adverse outcome. Having parents with untreated and significant ADHD, where there are poor family relationships and inconsistent child-rearing habits, exacerbates a poor outcome. Similarly, living in an isolated family with continuing financial, housing or employment difficulties, and where there is little support from the school and others, exacerbates the outcome difficulties. However, factors that may improve the outcome include having milder core ADHD symptoms, fewer complications, a higher IQ and being diagnosed earlier in life.

When the diagnosis of ADHD is not made until teenage years, where the adolescent has progressed through puberty and had entered the more complex field of senior school, the outcome again appears to be worse. Then, the disruptive behaviour difficulties are often magnified, social skills difficulties make the progression into substance misuse or antisocial behaviour much more likely and increased demoralisation means it is frequently difficult to engage the adolescent in effective management.

Youth with the hyperactive form of ADHD who have the early onset of disruptive behaviour disorder, especially if there is associated mood instability, are much more likely to enter the youth justice system. For this to have happened represents a failure on the part of educational and medical systems. It is not only tragic for a person with such a treatable condition to have been allowed to progress this far, but it is also a reflection on society and the failure of these systems to have adequately protected the child. While adolescents within the youth justice system *can* still be treated for ADHD, it is much more difficult, and the ravages of the environment are greatly increased by that stage.

Positive features of ADHD

It is always important, however, to remember the positive attributes of the child. Parents almost always note their child's positive characteristics, which may have become blurred or lost by the ADHD difficulties. With treatment, these positive attributes can be turned to the individual's advantage. It is therefore important to reframe the ADHD once it is managed effectively. This is a very important part of management, especially in adolescence. The long-term educational, social, relationship and other goals often change to an extent not previously thought possible. Once a child with ADHD is able to complete school and start on further education or employment in an area of interest, the ability to over-focus and be extremely energetic can lead to great success.

Table 8.1 Factors affecting the outlook for people with ADHD (modified from H. Nash, *Kids, Families and Chaos*, Torrensville, S. Australia: Ed Med Publishers, 1996)

	Supporting factors	Hindering factors
Children:	■ milder core symptoms ■ few complications ■ early diagnosis ■ high IQ ■ predominantly inattentive ADHD	■ severe core symptoms ■ many complications ■ late diagnosis ■ low IQ ■ early-onset ODD or CD ■ Asperger's Syndrome
Parents:	■ ADHD absent or resolved ■ no psychiatric or social problems ■ high IQ ■ good family relationships ■ child-rearing consistent and supportive	■ ADHD unresolved ■ psychiatric or social problems ■ lower IQ ■ poor family relationships
Environment:	■ supportive extended family ■ no financial, employment or housing problems ■ school co-operation and support	■ isolation from family ■ financial, employment or housing problems ■ no school support

Positive attributes in the workplace of adults with ADHD:

- tend to think across boundaries;

- may be creative and work unconventionally;

- may be intuitive;

- often use their ability to over-focus to great advantage.

As adults, people with ADHD have many adaptive characteristics. They tend to think across boundaries and devise new ways of doing things. Because they get bored easily, they tend not to stay with any one thing for very long. They are able to switch their attention from one thing to another, and often have many things on the go at one time. They tend to see things not noticed by others, and they are generally fairly intuitive. However, their disorganisation can make them appear somewhat chaotic. Working within conventional systems or rules is not always easy and often they will achieve goals by somewhat unconventional means.

Especially if adequately treated, adults with ADHD can be delightful individuals with many endearing characteristics. However, untreated ADHD wreaks havoc on the lives of many, and is responsible for a wide range of difficulties including relationship problems, dysfunctional families, drug and alcohol abuse and employment difficulties, to name a few.

CASE STUDY   **Tom: a real-life story (written with Anne Douglas)**

The early years

As a toddler and a preschooler, Tom raced through the surface of life like a runaway train, scattering people and objects as he went. His energy levels were incredible. New toys, new people and new situations never satisfied him for long and everything was a battle. He never learnt from his mistakes, had no sense of danger and bumps and bruises were the norm. The day always began from the moment he woke with his insatiable demands. No one was prepared to babysit because he was so exhausting and it was no fun to take him anywhere. We wondered where we were going wrong.

His parents said:

- 'He never wanted a cuddle.'

- 'How could our lives be dictated to by such a small being?'

- 'We just went from one crisis to another.'

The health visitor said:

- 'He's not hyperactive because he slept all right.'

- 'You really needed to be firmer with him and not let him get away with so much.'

- 'Try giving him a soothing bath at midnight, if he's active all evening.'

The playgroup said:

- 'He's a real live wire and obviously only here for the social side of things.'

Family friends say:

- 'Boys are like that, he'll grow out of it.'

The GP said:

- 'He's just hyperactive; he'll grow out of it by puberty.'

- 'I'll arrange counselling for you if you like.'

The school years

By the time Tom goes to school his parents are reading all the parenting books they can get their hands on and are desperately trying to find better ways of dealing with him. Relationships are becoming very strained as he constantly confronts and defies the most reasonable efforts to improve his behaviour. Everyday tasks are a struggle. His hypersensitivity creates constant tension. He is over-competitive and possessive and regularly quarrels with his brother and friends.

His school reports poor concentration, laziness, easy distractibility and disorganisation and complains of class clowning and uncompleted homework and other tasks. However, they feel he has the potential to do better. They clearly expect his parents to improve the situation and they question their discipline.

Life becomes one long round of arguments and tantrums from morning till night. Tom is permanently volatile and easily gets angry. Everyday life and holidays have to be geared to his needs as, unless he is happy, no-one else gets any peace. His parents are at their wits' end to know where to turn for help, ashamed to admit that they do not know how to bring up their own son. His brother, whom they treat the same way, seems to behave more appropriately, but it is clear that Tom reacts differently in every situation.

His parents say:

- 'He is so single-minded, he almost doesn't seem to have a conscience.'
- 'He uses "No" all the time, but doesn't respond to it himself.'
- 'He doesn't appreciate the effect his volatile actions have on the family.'
- 'When he occasionally slows down long enough to communicate, you can see the lost soul beneath the layers of chaos.'

His teachers say:

- 'He is just lazy, disorganised and forgetful.'
- 'No amount of reward or punishment makes any difference.'
- 'Tom doesn't seem to understand cause and effect.'

His brother says:

- 'He tries to dominate everything – it's always his rules.'

Family friends say:

- 'You're over-protecting.'

The years 18–24

Exam results were naturally disappointing as life progressively deteriorated for Tom. The lack of structure in further education led to poor attendance, incomplete work, missed deadlines and failed assignments. Disorganisation and chaos dominated his existence. Money slipped through his fingers as he endlessly sought new stimulation to beat the constant boredom he felt. His whole existence was a disaster and it was difficult to envisage any kind of future for him, yet he still resisted attempts for help. He went from job to job without direction, finding everything too boring and not being able to concentrate long enough to learn new things. Gradually, he realised that he was being left behind by his brother and friends, as they began new stages of their lives. However, there was one positive outcome to this catalogue of despondency: starting work forced him to acknowledge his own problems and, at last, he was motivated to take some action.

His parents say:

- 'His problems certainly didn't stop once he was a teenager, as the books said they would.'
- 'He puts off everything till later.'
- 'We can't really see him ever becoming really independent or mature.'

His brother says:

- 'He leaves a trail of chaos; his bedroom has to be seen to be believed.'
- 'It's hard to remember any good times we shared.'
- 'My parents always had different rules for him – it wasn't fair.'

His friends say:

- 'He loses interest in things so quickly.'

His employers say:

- 'His timekeeping is appalling.'
- 'He has had so many jobs already.'

Now (age 25)

Although his parents realised eight years ago that he almost certainly had ADHD, he would only accept advice recently and was only then formally diagnosed. The change in his demeanour has been remarkable since he embarked on the treatment for his ADHD. He confided to his mother that he used to think he was a freak. The treatment has allowed him to be reflective for the first time and he is happier about himself as he now participates in his life instead of it controlling him. He says he feels more confident, enjoys being more responsible and is keen to get on with his life and make up for lost time. He now realises how much his inability to concentrate hindered him throughout school. Instead of criticism, accusation and rejection he now gets encouragement, praise and acceptance for his achievements, both at work and leisure. Previously, apart from his talent at football, his poor concentration, boredom and impulsiveness have prevented him from trying or accomplishing anything new.

He is motivated to continue with his treatment because he recognises that it works. There is no doubt that he clearly needs his medication. Both he and his family are acutely aware if he misses a dose or when they have worn off. The quality of his life is so much better and he can start to build on his successes.

For almost 25 years Tom's life had been utterly chaotic and distressing both to himself and those who care about him. Those outside the family who were involved with him had little time for his volatile, immature and unreasonable behaviour, yet underneath it all one sensed there was a lost soul, desperately trying to feel normal. His courage in finally confronting his problems and accepting the necessary help has unlocked a likeable and enthusiastic personality, with great potential. Of course, it will not all be plain sailing and there are bound to be setbacks. However, where once he had no future, at last he has the chance to fulfil his potential.

His GP said:

- 'This ADHD thing is just an American fad.'
- 'I've never heard of adult ADHD.'
- 'I wouldn't prescribe a dangerous medication anyway.'

The specialist says:

- 'He has long-standing severe ADHD. I can't understand why he hasn't even been treated for his hyperactivity before now. He also has ODD and OCD. The most effective help for him is medication and I would recommend an appropriate trial.'

Tom says:

- 'I've never really known what it was like to concentrate before.'
- 'I have so much to catch up on in my life to make up for lost time.'
- 'I realise I never revised for exams because I just couldn't get started and it was too boring.'
- 'I've now read my first book from cover to cover; before, I couldn't even take in the first line.'
- 'I got my driving licence when I was 18 but never had the confidence to drive. Now I've started again.'
- 'Work is going so well.'
- 'I've got my first girlfriend.'
- 'I'm able to try new things and am no longer afraid of failing.'

His brother says:

- 'He is calmer and more interested in others.'
- 'He is much better company and a real friend now.'

His parents say:

- 'He is perceptive and thoughtful now; he even thinks about others and shows appreciation.'
- 'We can see a future for him now; at last he has a chance of making the most of his opportunities and realising that he is, after all, lovable and effective.'

9 Concluding comments

The existence of ADHD is now well beyond debate. In the UK it was validated by the report of the National Institute of Clinical Excellence in 2000, and developed further with a review in 2004 and reinforced in 2008. The management of ADHD is definitely being incorporated into expectations of the Health Service by clinical governance, and also into the educational service, especially by the Children's National Service Framework and by the Government's strategy for special educational needs – *Removing Barriers to Achievement* (2004).

The condition is managed both by paediatricians and psychiatrists within child and adolescent mental health services; close integration between these services and educational services is important. There is now a general recognition that the condition is not just about severe hyperactivity but also about the broader concept of ADHD, which includes inattentiveness and impulsiveness. The importance of coexisting conditions in determining clinical presentation and in predicting outcome is also respected.

There is also increased recognition and understanding of the reality of ADHD, and commissioning of children's services increasingly acknowledges this. The earlier scepticism about the very existence of ADHD and about the medications frequently used to treat it has largely now been replaced by an awareness of the importance of ADHD in the special educational needs framework and in society generally. The pseudo-controversy largely caused by the myth and misinformation from those not understanding ADHD continues, but it is generally minimised now.

There is still, however, a lot of progress to be made in the management of the condition in adolescents and adults, and especially those at risk of entering the criminal justice system. The fact that a high percentage of people within the youth justice system have untreated ADHD, and have progressed untreated through school, raises a great many issues regarding better provision of mental health services for the youth justice, and indeed, criminal justice systems.

There will always be much more to learn about ADHD, but this should not detract from the reality of the condition, nor prevent us from applying the knowledge we already have to the effective treatment of adults and children. Children with ADHD are not 'problem children' but children who have a problem. Unrecognised and untreated ADHD prevents a happy childhood and blights a future.

The families of children with ADHD deserve support and understanding, not blame. The increasing evidence that ADHD is a biological deficit in impulse control, and thus in self-control, goes to the heart of commonly held societal beliefs of self-responsibility and is one of the main reasons for controversy surrounding ADHD.

However, the effects of ADHD need to be experienced to be truly understood. The condition deserves to be taken much more seriously. It is vital that all professionals

> Studies suggest that between 50% and 70% of young people within the youth justice system may have untreated ADHD.

involved with children be open-minded, become informed and acknowledge the existence and reality of ADHD and their role in providing essential management and support. Teachers can make such a positive difference to these children with effective management of their difficulties and by fully understanding the condition. Children with ADHD and their families should expect nothing less.

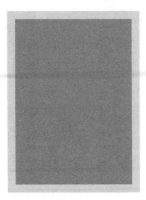

Appendix 1: Further reading

All of these books are available on the ADDISS website, www.addiss.co.uk, as well as books on other conditions.

Attwood, T. (1998) *Asperger's Syndrome: A Guide for Parents and Professionals*. Jessica Kingsley Publications.

Barkley, R.A. (1998) *Attention Deficit Hyperactivity Disorder: A Handbook for Diagnosis and Treatment*. Guilford Press.

Barkley, R.A. (1998) *Taking Charge of ADHD: The Complete Authoritative Guide for Parents*. Guilford Press.

Brooks, R. and Goldstein, G. (2001) *Raising Resilient Children*. New York: Contemporary.

Brown, T. (2000) *Attention Deficit Disorders and Comorbidities in Children, Adolescents and Adults*. American Psychiatric Press.

Cowne, E. (2003) *The SENCO Handbook* (4th edn). David Fulton Publishers.

Dendy, C.Z. (1995) *Teenagers with ADD: A Parents' Guide*. Woodbine House.

Dendy, C.Z. (2000) *Teaching Teens with ADD and ADHD*. Woodbine House.

Kewley, G. (1995) 'Medical aspects of the assessment and treatment of children with ADD', in Cooper, P. and Ideus, K. (eds), *Association of Workers for Children with Emotional and Behavioural Difficulties*, pp. 31–7.

Nadeau, K.G., Littman, E. and Quinn, P. (1999) *Understanding Girls with ADHD*. Advantage Books.

National Institute for Clinical Excellence (2008) *Guidance on the Use of Methylphenidate for Attention Deficit/Hyperactivity Disorder (ADHD) in Childhood*, 66, 715–30.

Stoddart, K.P. (2005) *Children, Youth and Adults with Asperger Syndrome: Integrating Multiple Perspectives*. Jessica Kingsley Publication.

Wilens, T.E. (2004) *Straight Talk About Psychiatric Medications for Kids*. Guilford Press.

Parents

Brown, T. (2006) *ADD: The Unfocused Mind*. Yale University Press.

Kewley, Dr G.D. (2001) *ADHD: Recognition, Reality and Resolution*. David Fulton.

Kutscher, M.L. (2009) *ADHD, Living without Brakes*. Jessica Kingsley.

Lawlis, Dr F. (2005) *ADD Answer*. Viking Studios.

Phelan, T. (1996) *1–2–3 Magic* (2nd edn). Child Management Inc.

Phelan, T. (2003) *Self Esteem Resolutions in Children*. Child Management Inc.

Children

Alexander-Roberts, C. (1995) *ADHD and Teens*. Taylor Publishing Company.

Galvin, M. (2001) *Otto Learns about His Medicine*. American Psychological Association.

Gehret, J. (2009) *Eagle Eyes*. Verbal Images Press.

Gehret, J. and De Pauw, S.A. (1996) *The Don't Give Up Kid*. Verbal Images Press.

Gordon, M. (1991) *I Would if I Could: A Teenagers' Guide to ADHD*. Atlantic Books.

Hoopman, K. (2008) *All Dogs Have ADHD*. Jessica Kingsley.

Leigh, J. (2005) *Zak Has ADHD*. Red Kite Books.

Moser, A. (2001) *Don't be a Menace on Sundays*, series based on the days of the week. Landmark Editions.

Parker, R. (1995) *Slam Dunk: A Young Boy's Struggle with ADHD*. Partners Publishing Group.

Quinn, P.O. and Stern, J.M. (2009) *Putting on the Brakes*. Magination Press.

Taylor, B. (2008) *ADHD and Me* (1st edn). New Harbinger Publications, US.

Yemula, Dr R.C. (2006) *Everything a Child Needs to Know About ADHD*. ADDISS.

Siblings

Gordon, M. (2004) *My Brother is a First Class Pain*. Jessica Kingsley Publishers.

Adults

Anderton, P. (2008) *The Tipping Points*. ADDISS.

Hallowell, E. (1995) *Driven to Distraction*. Touchstone.

Kolberg, J. (2002) *ADD Friendly Ways to Organise Your Life*. Routledge.

Nadeau, K. (1995) *Understanding Women with ADD*. Touchstone.

Nadeau, K. (1997) *ADD in the Workplace*. Routledge.

Patterson, K. (2004) *ADD and Me*. Jessica Kingsley Publishers.

Sarkis, S. (2009) *ADD and Your Money*. New Harbinger Publications.

Solden, S. (2005) *Women with ADD* (2nd edn). Underwood Books Inc.

Appendix 2: Useful addresses

ADD Information Services
The ADDISS Resource Centre
PO Box 340
Edgware
Middlesex
HA8 9HL
Tel: 020 8906 9068
Fax: 020 8959 0727
Email: info@addiss.co.uk

www.addiss.co.uk – Produces a wide range of books on ADHD and related subjects. Helpful information and advice and details of local support groups.

Advisory Centre for Education (ACE)
Unit 1B Aberdeen Studios
22 Highbury Grove
London
N5 2DQ
Tel: 020 7354 8321

British Dyslexia Association
98 London Road
Reading
RG1 5A
Tel: 0118 966 8271

Independent Panel for Special Educational Advice (IPSEA)
22 Warren Hill Road
Woodbridge
Suffolk
IP12 4DU
Tel: 01394 382814

National Autistic Association
393 City Road
London
EC1V 1NG
Tel: 020 7833 2299

OAASIS
Brock House
Grigg Lane
Brockenhurst
Hants
SO42 7RE

Learning Assessment & Neurocare Centre
48–50 Springfield Road
Horsham
West Sussex
RH12 2PD
Tel: 01403 240002
Fax: 01403 260900
Email: info@lanc.uk.com www.lanc.uk.com

A multidisciplinary clinic for assessment and management of children and adults
with neurodevelopmental, behavioural and learning difficulties, especially ADHD
and related conditions.

National Resource Centre on ADHD – US CHADD
8181 Professional Place
Suite 150
Landover
Maryland 20785
www.help4adhd.org; www.chadd.org

The Dyspraxia Trust
PO Box 3
Hitchin
Herts
SG5 1UU
Tel: 01462 454986

Tourette Syndrome (UK) Association
PO Box 26149
Dunfermline
KY12 7YU
Tel: 0845 458 1252

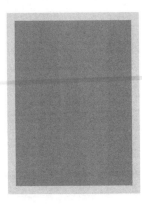

Index